# TURKEY HUNTING

PRO TACTICS™ SERIES

# TURKEY HUNTING

*Use the Secrets of the Pros to
Bag More Birds*

## Bob Humphrey

THE LYONS PRESS

Guilford, Connecticut

An imprint of The Globe Pequot Press

The Lyons Press is an imprint of The Globe Pequot Press.

Pro Tactics is a trademark of Morris Book Publishing, LLC.

Photos © Bob Humphrey unless otherwise credited
Project manager: Julie Marsh
Text designer: Peter Holm (Sterling Hill Productions) and Libby Kingsbury
Layout artist: Kim Burdick

Library of Congress Cataloging-in-Publication data is available.
Humphrey, Bob.
   Turkey hunting : use the secrets of the pros to bag more birds / Bob Humphrey.
      p. cm.
   Includes index.
   ISBN 978-1-59921-202-9
   1. Turkey hunting. 2. Wild turkey. I. Title.
   SK325.T8H858 2009
   799.2'4645--dc22
                                    2009003116
Printed in China

10 9 8 7 6 5 4 3 2 1

The author and The Globe Pequot Press assume no liability for accidents happening to, or injuries sustained by, readers who engage in the activities described in this book.

# CONTENTS

# FOREWORD

I was twelve years old, riding out of a southeastern Virginia swamp in the back of a pickup truck following a deer hunt, the first time I ever saw a wild turkey. There were two of them, and I couldn't tell you whether they were hens or young gobblers or perhaps even a pair of mature toms. They stepped into the muddy, rutted logging road just after the truck passed and with heads down marched across the open lane before disappearing behind an exposed clump of roots from a toppled cypress tree.

The other hunters in the truck, a mix of several men and boys, began chatting in disbelief. In those days spotting a turkey was as uncommon, and almost as unbelievable, as a Bigfoot sighting. I wouldn't see another one until joining a friend on a real turkey hunt almost eleven years later.

That friend, James Ramsey, a firefighter, had hunted turkeys for the first time the year before. With the weekdays off that his job afforded, he was determined to give it another go but preferred to have somebody join him in his effort. The problem was he didn't have anybody else who could, or would, go with him during the week; most folks were working. In my twenties and recently graduated from college, I was still waiting tables in an upscale Virginia Beach restaurant, reluctant to give up the good nightly tips for the paltry weekly paycheck a fledgling news reporter would make at a small weekly or daily paper. Consequently, my days were open.

I have to confess that nothing in my prior experience had particularly inspired me to want to hunt turkeys. I never saw any when I hunted deer or small game back then, other than that one time already mentioned. In fact, when my friend first asked me if I wanted to join him, I was as skeptical as if I had just been asked to join a group of people on a nighttime snipe hunt — as many of you know, a traditional opportunity to trick the uninitiated into heading into the dark woods for a nonexistent bird and then leaving them, usually lost and terrified, behind. I imagined we would have about as much luck finding a wild turkey as the unlucky victim would finding a snipe.

Yet I agreed. If nothing else, it was a good excuse to get out in the woods at a time of year that I wasn't typically out there. And finding time to spend outdoors is never a bad idea.

Little did I realize then, but that first trip would launch me on a thrilling yet unexpected course that has enriched many aspects of my life. We didn't get a tom on that trip; I didn't even glimpse one, but I did, for the first time, hear a gobble. And every time that sharp, rattling sound echoed off the trees around me, it held me spellbound. It was enough to ignite a fire in my soul that only grows and joyously consumes me each spring and, increasingly, each fall season as well.

I'd love to say I filled a tag my first year of hunting. Or the next. Or the next. But I didn't. And James didn't, either. It was like the blind leading the blind through an ever-changing obstacle course, though, despite many days of frustration, I'd be lying if I said I didn't have a lot of fun navigating those unfamiliar turkey woods. I enjoyed a number of close encounters in those first years, getting gobblers to respond to my amateurish calls and even pulling them close enough to present me with a look at them in all their strutting glory. But I just never could seem to work them those last 20 or 30 yards into shotgun range. It took me five years before I finally coaxed one to the gun.

As I read through this book for the first time, it occurred to me that I wish Bob Humphrey had written it a lot earlier; I could have used it back then.

I first became familiar with Bob's keen knowledge of turkeys during my time as editor of *Turkey Call* magazine, published by the National Wild Turkey Federation, where I worked for nearly seven years. Bob was already a frequent contributor to the publication when I arrived, and the manner in which he was able to share his experiences and help other hunters find success was a welcome addition to any issue of the magazine.

Even as my own turkey-hunting experience grew and I moved on to *Outdoor Life* and began blogging on the magazine's Web site about turkey hunting, I still found Bob a reliable source of help for answers to some of the questions posed by readers that I wasn't sure about and a great guy to bounce ideas off. Trained in wildlife biology, he knows the hows, wheres, and whys of turkey behavior and habitat. And it is from that vein that Bob has helped other hunters improve their days in the woods.

But what makes him truly effective in sharing his message and making this book in particular such a useful resource for hunters regardless of their skill level is his ability to cut through the jargon and scientific mumbo-jumbo that drives readers (and editors) crazy. He still delivers all the hard-hitting information needed with the thoroughness of a biologist but in a way that makes it read like a good story rather than a textbook.

From preparing for the hunt and understanding how to find, set up on, and call wild turkeys to what to do after you successfully have put one on the ground, *Pro Tactics: Turkey Hunting* leaves no aspect of the hunt unturned. It's a manual worthy of keeping within close reach of your fireside easy chair or even tucking into your turkey vest for quick reference in the field.

Whether you're still trying to figure out this sport or you're a vet of countless turkey seasons, when you run up against a tough tom, you can sometimes use a spark of input from a fellow hunter to help kindle a game plan that will work. With this book within reach, Bob's many years of hunting wild turkeys across the United States will be there to provide that spark.

Doug Howlett
Editor, *Southern Sporting Journal*
Southampton County, Virginia
August 2008

# ACKNOWLEDGMENTS

Though the cover of this book bears my name, preparing it was hardly a singular effort—far from it. In some ways it involves everyone who has ever shared the turkey woods with me. They are too numerous to name—you know who you are.

I must also thank the many gun, call, apparel, and other outdoor-product companies, their pro staffers and PR/marketing reps for providing invaluable information and opportunities to hunt the greatest game bird with some of the most knowledgeable and experienced turkey hunters in the world.

Last but not least, I must thank my devoted wife, Jane, for her patience, understanding, and support during my frequent absences in the spring and fall; and my newest hunting partners, Helen and Ben (my kids), for rekindling the hunting spirit.

# Hunters of the New Millennium

When I sat down and began planning out this book, I thought to myself, "How can I make it something different, something more than just another turkey-hunting book? How can I provide something useful and innovative?" The first step was to study other books to see what they had and what they lacked. They all seemed pretty thorough and comprehensive when it came to how to hunt turkeys; and the techniques, the substance of turkey hunting, haven't changed all that much.

However, the face of turkey hunting has changed dramatically in just the last ten years or so. We now have more birds on this continent than ever existed in history, or prehistory for that matter. The challenge of finding birds to hunt has been replaced with the challenge of finding accessible land to hunt them on. We now have to outwit both our quarry and other hunters.

Technological advancements in clothing, ammunition, optics, and electronics have provided the modern turkey hunter with a world of new equipment options. These tools are designed not to make the hunt any easier or less challenging. Rather, they are intended to make us safer, more comfortable, more effective, and more efficient at making a clean, ethical kill.

The element of fair chase remains firmly intact.

While the quarry hasn't changed, the hunter has. Today's turkey hunter is different. We're more educated because we have a vastly larger pool of information from which to draw. Life is much more fast paced. The modern hunter has less time and more means, so we seek out efficiencies.

With the boon in turkey numbers, today's hunters are also voluntarily seeking more and greater challenges. We continue to create ever more complex goals for ourselves: grand slams, royal slams, world slams, Mexican and Canadian slams. Interest in bowhunting turkeys has skyrocketed.

Hunting birds in the local woodlot is no longer enough. More and more of us are traveling across the country, attempting to quench our insatiable thirst to pursue the king of North American game birds—a virtually unattainable goal.

It was with all this in mind that I finally began tapping on the keyboard. My goal: to produce a comprehensive and, more importantly, contemporary guidebook for turkey hunters of the new millennium. Of course, no such tome would be complete without substantial reverence and reference to the tools and techniques that got us to where we are today. I have attempted to meld these seamlessly into a timeless, yet current manual that will provide valuable information for both novice and veteran.

As with anything I do related to the grand pastime of turkey hunting, it was a labor of love. I hope that you will enjoy reading it as much as I did writing it and that you'll find some valuable piece of information in here that somehow, someday, will make your hunt more successful and, most importantly, more enjoyable.

# PART I:
# PREPARATION

# CHAPTER ONE

# The Wild Turkey

The memory fades a little with each passing year, but if I close my eyes and let my mind wander, I can still recall my first bird.

It was nearing the end of yet another frustrating turkey season. I'd spent most of the previous three days just looking for birds, with little success. On a whim a friend and I did an afternoon windshield tour of several nearby towns, eventually locating what looked like some good turkey ground. A little more on-foot scouting confirmed that turkeys had been in the area recently. The question was, how recently? A day? A week? A month?

I arrived the following morning in the dark and started into the woods with little expectation and no particular destination in mind. By this time I was just going through the motions. Mentally, I'd all but given up, and physically, I was a wreck. My feet were sore from miles of hiking, and my eyelids were heavy from too many early mornings.

That all changed in a heartbeat with the sound of a distant gobble. My heart raced, and the soreness and fatigue vanished, as if by magic. I waited for one more gobble, took a bearing, and tore off on a hundred-yard dash. I stopped long enough to catch my breath and another gobble and was off to the races again. One more sprint put me as close as I dared go. It was time to make a stand.

Frantically, I searched for a likely ambush spot, fearing the bird would appear at any moment and catch me standing in the open. There! The base of a big oak would provide a perfect backrest. I hastily nestled in, propped my gun up, and prepared to call.

I popped in a diaphragm call, pushed it to the roof of my mouth, and got ready. The call fit the roof of my mouth like a glove. I'd practiced with it for hours, mimicking the cassette that came with it until I sounded just like Ray Eye and Tom Stuckey. Only this time when I pushed air over its surface nothing happened. My mouth was bone dry, and the call wouldn't work.

I fought with every fiber of my being to calm myself, eventually mustering up enough spit to make a few loud yelps. To my utter amazement the bird gobbled back. I called again; he gobbled again, this time closer. The game was on.

Eventually, the bird's gobbling reached a fevered pitch. I called again but this time got no response. Suddenly the woods seemed eerily silent. I fought the temptation to move, instead straining my ears for any sound. "What was that?" A strange bass noise, like the hum of distant traffic, then soft footsteps on the dry leaves. He was close now, very close.

Again I fought the temptation to move, which was made all the harder by deteriorating conditions. My heart pounded, and my legs began to quiver. Mosquitoes, attracted by the sudden surge of carbon dioxide in the air, stung the flesh around my eyes, nose, and lips at will. Still, I did not move.

There it was again, a booming drone resonating from deep within the chest of a wild tom turkey. Then more footsteps. I could make out location now and direction. He was circling around behind my

■ The Eastern is the largest and most widespread subspecies of wild turkey, occurring in all states east of the Mississippi River and ranging west into eastern portions of the plains states and Texas.

left shoulder, past a large pile of slash. I had no choice. Being a right-handed shooter, I had to move.

I tried to time it so the bird would be obscured behind the slash pile when I turned. I spun around, aiming my gun where I thought he would emerge, and my eyes scanned quickly for the bird. Nowhere. No, wait. There he is.

I nearly fainted at the sight of his glowing red, white, and blue head and his iridescent copper and black feathers from a mere 20 yards' distance. A beady black eye stared menacingly at me. I was sure he saw me, but if he did, he showed no reaction. Then it was over.

I squeezed the trigger, the gun went off, and the bird disappeared behind the slash pile. Though numb from immobility, I somehow managed to vault upright and sprint toward him. As I peered around the slash, I saw him there in his death throes. He was magnificent. I'd finally met the wild turkey.

Since then I've become obsessed with turkeys. I spend countless hours in the woods each spring and fall pursuing them. Between seasons I watch and photograph them and read every piece of literature I can put my hands on. All this has made me a better hunter.

While you don't need to be obsessed to be successful, I firmly believe that the more you learn about your quarry, the more successful you'll be at hunting it. This includes success both in filling your tags and in better understanding what you're observing in the field. There's a lot to learn about turkey hunting—but let's learn a little about the turkeys themselves first.

## What Is a Turkey? The Basics

Basically, a turkey is just a big chicken, characterized by strong legs and feet, which are used to scratch for food; short, rounded wings designed for brief, rapid flight; and a short, stout beak for pecking.

The turkey's brain is about the size of a walnut—not the whole nut, just the meat inside. More often than not, however, they still manage to elude us. You can console yourself in knowing that it is not intelligence but instinct, honed over eons of living in the wild, that is the turkey's greatest asset—that and its keen senses.

It is sometimes said that if turkeys could smell, you'd never kill them. While their sense of smell is poor, they more than make up for it with keen eyesight and hearing. It is not so much magnification but the rate at which they can assimilate detail and detect movement that accounts for the turkey's legendary eyesight. Additionally, their stationary field of vision encompasses 300 degrees. A slight turn of the head allows for 360 degrees. Just as important is the fact they can distinguish color extremely well.

Their hearing is also acute. Studies suggest that they can hear in the subsonic and supersonic range, below and above the range in which humans hear. And they can hear for quite some distance. While it has yet to be proven scientifically, I've observed they're also remarkably adept at pinpointing the location of certain sounds. Coincidence alone cannot account for the number of times I've made a call and later—sometimes much later—had a turkey come to the precise location from which I made that call.

You need to know the difference between males and females, as virtually all spring turkey seasons are limited to males only. Simply stated, males are bigger and darker. Size varies with age, location, and race, but in general females are half to two-thirds the size of males. The body (or contour) feathers of males are black tipped, giving the birds an overall blackish color. Those of the females are buff tipped, making them appear more brownish.

In poor light the naked, nearly featherless heads of males and females can look similar. The female's is bluish gray in color, while that of the male is more red. During the breeding season, however, a male's head takes on a brilliant red, white, and blue hue. The front of his head is also adorned with a slender, fleshy appendage at the base of the bill. Called a "snood," it becomes elongated and dangles beside the head when the bird is excited.

Males have two other physical characteristics you can use to distinguish them from hens (sometimes).

Nearly all males sport a beard—an appendage of modified feathers that dangles from the bird's breast. Beards grow

roughly 3 to 5 inches a year. A one-year-old male sporting a beard of this length is called a "jake." The beard of a two-year-old male is typically 8 to 10 inches, and from this point on he is called a "tom." For the first three years, a gobbler's beard will be amber tipped. After that, it will appear entirely black. The beard continues to grow throughout the gobbler's life, though growth slows in later years and the ends begin to wear off.

In northern regions beard tips may allegedly become encrusted with ice and break off (though no one's actually demonstrated or observed this). Some birds will experience "beard rot," a malady believed to be from a parasitic infection. Such beards are often shorter, and the ends appear frayed and lighter in color. In these cases beard length is not a reliable indicator of age.

It's important to note that roughly 4 percent of hens sport beards, and gobblers may occasionally lack them altogether. Typically, a gobbler has one beard, though some may sport several. According to records from the National Wild Turkey Federation, the record for the most beards ever seen on a single bird is nine.

Males sport spurs on the back of their lower legs; females generally lack them. In addition to differentiating males from females, they are also a somewhat reliable indicator of age. Subadult males (jakes) typically have short, rounded spurs of $\frac{1}{2}$ inch or less, while those of a two-year-old generally range from $\frac{5}{8}$ to $\frac{7}{8}$ inch. At age

## Characteristics of the Wild Turkey

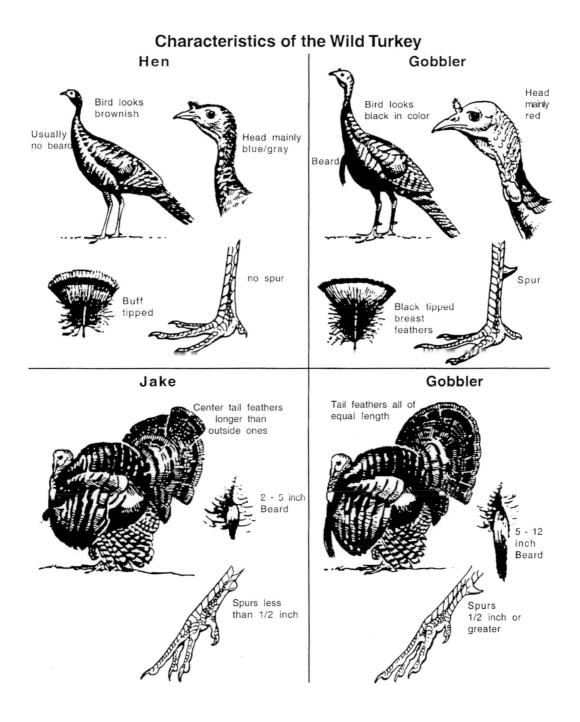

Hen — Bird looks brownish; Usually no beard; Head mainly blue/gray; Buff tipped; no spur

Gobbler — Bird looks black in color; Head mainly red; Beard; Black tipped breast feathers; Spur

Jake — Center tail feathers longer than outside ones; 2 - 5 inch Beard; Spurs less than 1/2 inch

Gobbler — Tail feathers all of equal length; 5 - 12 inch Beard; Spurs 1/2 inch or greater

■ By their second spring young males, or "jakes," typically sport a beard that is 3 to 5 inches long. Their spurs are little more than hobnails, and the central feathers of their tail fans are noticeably longer than the others. COURTESY OF THE NATIONAL WILD TURKEY FEDERATION

three a tom may have spurs of 1 inch or slightly longer. By age four the spurs may be 1¼ to 1½ inches long. As the spurs grow longer, they become sharper and more hooked.

There are five generally recognized subspecies or races of wild turkeys in the United States. The Eastern is the largest and most widespread, occurring in all states east of the Mississippi River and ranging west into eastern portions of the plains states and Texas. The Osceola (or Florida) turkey has the narrowest range, occurring in central and south Florida only. It differs from the Eastern in being somewhat smaller with much more dark barring in the primary wing feathers and longer, narrower spurs.

The Rio Grande turkey occupies a range that spans an area covering roughly from Kansas south through Texas and into northeastern Mexico, with scattered populations in California and Oregon. Transplanted populations also occur in California, Oregon, and Hawaii. The tips of its tail feathers and tail coverts (smaller

■ The Rio Grande turkey ranges over much of the lower Midwest and Texas, though isolated populations also occur in California, Oregon, and Hawaii.

■ The range of the Merriam's subspecies is scattered across the Northwest, Southwest, and mountain states.

feathers covering the tail base) tend to be lighter and more buff colored than those of the Eastern.

The Merriam's subspecies occurs from the Southwest north into Wyoming, Montana, and Idaho and west to Nevada, Washington, and Oregon. Its tail feathers and coverts are nearly white, and its gobble is slower and more high-pitched than that of the Eastern. Last but not least is the Gould's, which most closely resembles the Merriam's. It is more common in Mexico and is a peripheral species in the United States, with small populations ranging north into New Mexico.

## Behavior and Life History

You don't need to know everything about the turkey's life history and behavior, though almost everything you learn could ultimately contribute to success. There is, however, a lot you should know about the spring and fall habits of turkeys. Spring mating is perhaps the most important aspect of turkey behavior that hunters need to understand. Most of our hunting occurs in the spring and is based on the mating habits of turkeys.

## The Roost

The turkey's day begins well before dawn. The eastern sky has yet to turn a rosy pink when the birds begin stirring high among the limbs of their roost trees. And the woods are still dark when the first gobbles echo down the valley. Already we're learning something.

It's no accident that the birds choose the places they do to roost. Once you know what they're looking for, it becomes much easier for you to key in on roosts, which is where you'll want to start your day, too.

Roost sites vary geographically, but all have some things in common. In the forests of the Northeast and north-central United States, where choices are nearly unlimited, turkeys will roost most anywhere. However, they tend to key in on the largest softwood trees—particularly big white pines—which offer the most protection from predators and the elements. In the West and Southwest, turkeys have few if any choices. Whether it's live oaks in Texas or cottonwoods in Wyoming, they're limited to what few tall trees grow along the river or creek corridors. And though they have more choices in the Southeast, they show a propensity for roosting over water. This may be because it affords greater protection or simply because the larger hardwoods occur along river bottoms.

## Touchdown

Even before they hit the ground, males and females have two entirely different thoughts on their minds. For the hens it's food; for toms it's sex. In either case it will influence where they go. Hens will head for the nearest food source. Any accompanying toms will follow the hens.

Solo toms will try to seek out hens, but they do this in several ways. One is by gobbling, and they seem to know instinctively that their gobbles are best heard from higher locations. That's why in uneven terrain they'll often head for the high ground. Another way toms attract hens is by strutting, which is why toms also have a propensity to head for open areas. These could be as large as a hundred-acre food plot or as small as a log landing or skid road.

So often you read or hear that calling a tom to your location goes against nature. Let's put this misconception to roost once and for all. It's true that a tom gobbles and struts to attract a hen to his location. If she won't go to him, however, he will often quite willingly go to a hen—or to something he perceives as a hen. If this weren't true, we wouldn't be able to call turkeys.

## Food Habits

Let's go back to the hens for a moment. From the time they hit the ground until late morning, they're looking for one thing: food. Find the food, and you'll find the birds. However, it's difficult to get too specific on food habits because they vary so much with geography and season.

Basically, turkeys eat about what you'd expect. Plants and plant material make up as much as 85 percent of an adult turkey's diet. The young poults (young birds less than four or five months old), meanwhile, rely much more heavily on a protein-rich diet of insects to power their rapidly growing bodies. As they mature their diet gradually shifts from insects to succulent plants. Then in late summer both young and adult birds change their diets from succulent greens to hard and soft mast: seeds, nuts, and berries.

## The Mating Game

Knowing the turkey's mating strategy can also contribute to your success. Turkeys are polygamous, which means one tom mates with several hens and a hen may mate with several different toms. Generally, though, a tom gathers a harem, much like a bull elk would. And the more hens he has, the more difficult it becomes to call him away from them. To a tom a bird in the harem is worth two in the bush.

## Rivalry

Another important aspect of turkey behavior is social ranking. Like their smaller cousins the chickens, for which the term was coined, turkeys have a pecking order or dominance hierarchy. Every bird in the flock has a rank, either

above or below his or her flock mates. The process of establishing this order begins shortly after hatching but will change as birds move from family groups into adult groups segregated by sex and age.

For adult males the deck gets shuffled each spring. Prior to the mating season, males compete fiercely for higher rank and the privilege of doing most (but not all) of the breeding. Fighting persists during the breeding season, but that is most often among younger, subordinate birds. Still, it's

■ The Osceola, or Florida, subspecies of wild turkey is restricted to Florida, approximately from Orlando south.

good to know, because, just as with humans, nothing draws a crowd like a good fight.

### The Mating Cycle

You might wonder what things like clutch size and incubation period have to do with hunting. The answer, as it turns out, is quite a lot.

An adult hen typically lays a clutch of ten to twelve eggs, and it's a slow process. After mating she gradually becomes more solitary, eventually leaving the flock to lay a single egg. She then covers the egg with leaves and returns to the flock or moves off on her own to feed. She'll also roost with the rest of the flock in trees at night. The process is repeated as she lays roughly one egg a day in the same nest.

While there is considerable variation, hens usually sit for about an hour after laying each of their first five eggs. After the sixth they may remain for two hours. Sitting time increases with the laying of each subsequent egg. Once her clutch is complete (and nobody knows how she knows), the hen will incubate continuously, day and night, leaving the nest only for brief feeding recesses.

If a hen loses her nest or brood, she may start the breeding cycle all over again. Or she may simply give up and remain with the breeding flock throughout the entire spring hunting season.

### Tying It All Together

So why is all this stuff important? Let's use a typical flock (if there is such a thing) as an example. You've got one dominant tom, four subordinate longbeards, six jakes, and a dozen hens. At the beginning of the season, the alpha tom has what he wants, and he's not gonna leave it for your calls. However, one of the satellite toms might. If he's high in the pecking order, he may come running. If he's low, he may sneak in, fearing a trouncing by another more dominant male. The jakes, meanwhile, might trip over each other as they race to you.

As the hunting season progresses, those overanxious toms get weeded out (by your fellow hunters), leaving the more cautious or the more dominant birds. The scaredy-cats might still come, but it will take subtler coaxing. The boss is still holding with his girls.

But the harem is shrinking. Eventually, weather permitting, most or all of the girls will be off incubating, and one day the boss gobbler will wake up alone. He'll strike out looking for love, and for the first time all spring, he's vulnerable.

## Conclusion

These are but a few examples of why knowing your quarry is important; and it's just a primer on turkey biology and behavior. There's so much more to learn about these magnificent birds and how to hunt them. You can read about them in magazines and books like this; but there's no substitute for experience. In season or out, spend as much time as you can with them, and you won't be disappointed.

# CHAPTER TWO

# Gobbler Guns and Ammo

There was a time, not so long ago, when there was no such thing as a "turkey gun." We hunted turkeys with a shotgun, the same one we used for waterfowl or upland game and sometimes even deer. It had blued metal parts, wooden stocks, and a smoothbore barrel, usually between 28 and 30 inches long. That was all there was.

You couldn't buy a turkey gun; you had to invent one. My first began life as a basic Mossberg Model 500. I made sure no one was around (especially my parents) when I took the shiny new gun out of its box, brought it out back, and set it on the lawn. Then I took a can of green "bowflage" (camouflage paint) and spray painted the whole thing. After the green coat dried, I placed leaves and ferns randomly over its surface and sprayed a coat of brown paint. Then I removed the vegetation, stood back, and admired it; it was a work of art. Next I put on some after-market rifle sights—the kind intended for shooting slugs—to the rib. Finally, I added a sling.

It would be several more years before gun makers started taking turkey hunting seriously and designing guns specifically for that purpose. The first few who were bold enough to take the risk did just what I did. They spray painted their upland or waterfowl models and called them turkey guns; some added sights and slings. The concept took off, and soon everyone was making turkey guns.

It didn't take long for ammo makers to jump on the bandwagon. Interest in turkey hunting was skyrocketing, and they had an easy time convincing hunters: You have a turkey gun; you need turkey loads.

Conventional wisdom at the time recommended size 4 or 6 shot. Each has its pros and cons, which we'll discuss later. I used to reload my own shells, and one day I got a brainstorm: What if I put some of each—4s and 6s—in the same shell? Clearly I was a young man ahead of his time. Some of the first dedicated turkey loads were so-called duplex loads, containing two sizes of shot.

It wasn't merely marketing though; there was a certain logic to the ammo makers' argument. Previously, shotguns were intended largely to spray a pattern of shot over a broad area at a moving target. Turkey hunting, on the other hand, required guns and loads designed to deliver a large proportion of their pattern to a confined area, at a more or less stationary object.

Meanwhile, in 1991 the U.S. Fish and Wildlife Service banned the use of lead shot for waterfowl hunting. This had some unintended consequences that would prove a boon to turkey hunters. First, waterfowl hunters had to switch to steel shot. It had less energy and knockdown power than lead, so someone invented the 3-inch magnum. Then someone else reasoned, "If a 3-inch steel load could kill a goose, imagine what a 3-inch lead load could do to a turkey." Later, someone thought, "And what if you coated that lead with copper for even more hitting power?"

Turkey guns and loads were progressing, but there was still something missing. Unlike lead, steel shot required a more open choke (the restriction on the muzzle end of the barrel). Remember, the goal of

■ There are many choices, but the all-around standard turkey gun is a 12 gauge pump- or slide-action, chambered for 3¹/₂-inch magnum loads.

turkey hunting was a tighter pattern. And if tight was good, tighter must be better. Enter the super-full choke.

Ammo manufacturers countered with similar bigger-is-better logic, producing the 3½-inch shell.

Then the world of waterfowling offered one more unintentional gift. Younger gunners, who grew up using it, adapted well to steel shot. But old-timers despised and derided it. They longed for the good old days of 50- and 60-yard killing shots on geese. The ammo makers responded, producing shot from non-toxic alloys with much more down-range energy. Quite by accident, these new loads also produced much tighter patterns than steel or lead.

This brings us pretty much up to the present day. Modern turkey hunters have a broad array of vastly improved guns and ammo specifically designed for them. And that will be the focus of the remainder of this chapter. I'll offer up suggestions on what could work, but I'll focus on what will work the best and why. If you want to be successful, why not use the most effective tool?

I should also note that the focus will be on shotguns. I realize that some states permit the use of rifles and handguns for turkey hunting, and I have hunted turkeys with a rifle. However, I believe hunting turkeys with a long-range, single-projectile firearm is like pounding finish nails with a splitting maul. It'll work, but that's not what it's made for. The whole purpose of

turkey hunting is to call them in close and shoot 'em in the face.

## Setting the Standard

While there is no one right gun, there are some definite trends. Perhaps the easiest way to make recommendations for a turkey gun is to compare and contrast options against a standard. Because it's the most popular and widely used turkey gun, we'll use a 12 gauge slide-action, chambered for 3½-inch magnum loads, as our standard.

### Gauge

Let's start with the gauge. In the hands of an experienced and patient hunter, and with the right loads, the 20 gauge is certainly adequate. But even though "adequate" is not necessarily what we're after, the lighter recoil and smaller frame of the 20 gauge may make it a better option for younger hunters, women, small-framed men, or anyone sensitive to recoil. Just keep in mind that it will limit your effective range—substantially. I've patterned 20-gauge guns out to 40 yards on a range, under controlled conditions, and I even witnessed fellow outdoor writer John Phillips stone a bird at that range with one. But 25 yards is much more realistic and should be considered maximum by most people shooting a 20.

At the opposite end of the spectrum, as far as weight and recoil are concerned, is the 10 gauge. Old pal Gary Sefton wrote a song about his "three-and-a-half-inch ten-gauge magnum shotgun." And one of my old Alabama buddies, George Mayfield, used to hunt with an Ithaca Mag 10 he affectionately named Maggie.

They're both killin' machines. But with the tremendous advancements that have been made in both guns and ammo, you really don't gain much in killing power by staying with the 10. The 12-gauge 3½-inch magnum, which offers similar effective range and pattern density with slightly less weight and recoil, has rendered the 10 nearly obsolete as a turkey gun. Another significant advantage of the 12 is that you'll find far and away the most options in terms of make, model, and style.

## Action

Now on to action. First and foremost, I recommend some type of repeater. I've lost count of how many times I rolled a bird, only to have it recover and try to escape. The only time the bird did get away was when I didn't have a quick follow-up shot. Even though autoloaders offer roughly the same advantages as slide- or pump-actions in such situations, turkey hunters seem to prefer pumps for the same reasons waterfowlers do: There's less that can go wrong with them, and when it does, it's easier to fix. Double and single shots are obviously simpler and more reliable, but they offer more disadvantages than advantages. One notable exception, again, is with young or inexperienced hunters, where it's hard to beat a single-shot H&R.

## Choke

All modern turkey guns will accommodate interchangeable chokes. Which you should choose will depend to a large extent on what loads you shoot. The general rule of thumb used to be the tighter, the better, and it still is, for straight lead shot. Some of the newer nontoxic shot—like HEVI-Shot—is much harder than lead and patterns better in a more open choke. Other types, like Remington's Wingmaster HD, like a tighter choke. It's best to consult the manufacturer's recommendations and experiment.

## Chamber

In terms of chamber length, the advantages of a 3½ inch are so obvious I almost don't need to mention them. In a gun chambered for 3½ inch, you can shoot anything from a low-base 2¾ reduced-recoil load to a full-blown 3½-inch magnum gobbler thumper. That's a plus if you have one multipurpose gun or will be sharing it with other family members for whom recoil is an issue.

## Options

So far things have been fairly simple. The choices begin to get more complicated when you start looking at options, because there are so many. So let's look at them one by one.

### Finish

Surveys have shown color to be one of the most important factors a new-car buyer

■ Camo finish isn't absolutely necessary, but it definitely helps keep you concealed from sharp-eyed gobblers.

considers. While it doesn't directly affect the performance, the same is true, to a large extent, for a turkey gun. That's why most modern turkey guns come in camouflage, and you often have several choices from among the latest patterns. Does the pattern matter? Only to the shooter. Does the finish matter? Absolutely.

While not absolutely necessary, camo is best. Besides, it looks good. At a bare minimum you need a flat finish. You can get by with a black synthetic or unpolished, brown wooden stock and a plain, matte-finish barrel. Guns designed specifically for turkey hunting no longer come with a polished, blued barrel and receiver and a bowling-ball-finished stock, so you shouldn't have to resort to spray paint to dull an otherwise shiny finish that could spook game. If you do, a gun sock or no-mar tape may be a better option.

Now for stocks. Synthetic or wood? Here again, the choice is not critical. Many more turkey guns come standard with synthetic stocks, and they'll hold up better under the often-rigorous conditions.

Some folks like the aesthetics of a wood stock, though the drab birch stock of a turkey gun is usually only slightly more attractive than black synthetic. Still, you may save $10 or $20 by not going with camo.

Regardless, you'll want a good recoil pad, particularly if you're shooting heavy magnum loads. If your gun doesn't have one, there are plenty of good after-market versions available. And some of the newer turkey guns now come with recoil-reduction technology built into the stock.

Another recent trend in turkey guns is a rear stock with some type of pistol-grip design. Some are merely thumb-hole stocks, while others are more like an assault rifle. Because you aim a turkey gun like a rifle—you don't point it like a bird gun—this offers a firmer grip and more stable shooting platform. And it looks cool.

■ Some type of optical sight is well worth considering for your turkey gun. It'll magnify your target, help you concentrate on your point of aim, and help prevent those occasional misses.

### Sights

One of the broadest accessory categories is sights. And one of the biggest factors in what you choose is personal preference, though, again, some are better than others. The basic single-bead front sight is acceptable, but it only gives you one point of aim. The number-one reason for missing turkeys (at least those in range) is that the hunter lifts his cheek off the stock to peek over the barrel. The bead may still be on the bird but the gun is actually aimed over the bird's head.

Most turkey guns now come standard with fiber-optic rifle sights—one dot in the front, two in the rear. Having two points of aim helps keep your cheek on the stock, and the fiber optics glow in low light, making them easier to see. If your favorite turkey gun doesn't have one, pick up one of the myriad after-market jobs. There's also a litany of more complicated mechanical sighting devices you can affix to your barrel or receiver. All work, some better than others.

For many people an even better choice is an optical sight, and here too the options are numerous and varied. A simple red-dot scope gives you a single, illuminated reference point that's easy to find and get on target. A shotgun scope, meanwhile, offers magnification and a reticle (cross-hairs) for greater accuracy. Any type will do, but some now come with reticles designed specifically for turkey hunting. In any case, anything in the 2x-to-4x power range will suffice if you desire magnification. Rather than a wire reticle, some come with an illuminated red dot or holographic reticle in the center of the scope. Most of these lack magnification, but at 30 yards you don't really need it.

Yet another option is a Holosight. This device incorporates the same technology as the gun sight on a jet fighter. A circle-and-dot image is projected onto a small lens. Once you sight it in, no matter how you hold the gun or look through the sight, the red dot will be pointing at the target.

### Miscellaneous

A sling, while not necessary, is a very nice option that makes it easier to tote your gun around all day and frees up your hands to haul that big gobbler out of the woods at the end. If you have trouble holding up your gun when the moment of truth nears, consider affixing a mono- or bi-pod to your barrel. That way your gun will be up and ready when you need it, and you won't get fatigued.

## Ammo

Now it's on to what you put in your gun. We'll begin with the right shot size, a topic almost as contentious as deciding the best caliber for deer. Conventional wisdom says that sizes 4, 5, and 6 are among the best—though I know some hunters who use 2s and others that swear by 7½s.

Size 4 offers more knockdown power, while 6 offers a denser pattern. For years I used 5, as it offers a nice compromise.

However, with the advent of denser, heavier nontoxic loads like HEVI-Shot and Wingmaster HD, you can now go to a smaller shot size—such as 6—without sacrificing the energy of a 4.

While the aforementioned loads offer some very obvious advantages, good old lead still works just fine, and copper-plated lead works even better. Magnum loads offer more pellets, more powder, and more oomph. And pretty much all of what I call designer loads (designed specifically for turkeys) will kill a turkey well beyond a range you should be shooting them at.

## Patterning

The most important component of the whole system is not the ammo, or even the gun, but what you do with them . . . before you hunt. Regardless of what gauge, action, chamber, or shot size you select, you must pattern your gun before you hunt. First and foremost, it will tell you

■ Pattern your gun before you hunt with it. Start at 15 or 20 yards, and keep moving progressively back, in 5- or 10-yard increments. When you no longer have at least six to eight pellets in the vital area, you've exceeded your gun's effective range.

where your gun is shooting and if anything's off.

It also gives you a chance to fine-tune your system. If you're willing to devote the time and expense necessary, you may be astounded by the results. Every gun shoots a little differently, and different guns shoot different brands of ammo and different shot sizes differently. Not only that, but performance can vary considerably with different chokes, guns, and ammo. In some cases, standard 2¾-inch loads may actually pattern better than 3-inch loads in your gun. Or harder, copper-plated shot may pattern better in a full or modified choke than in a super-full turkey choke. You may find your gun patterns better with Winchester, Remington, or Federal ammunition. The only way to find out is to practice, before you hunt.

## Muzzleloaders

No discussion on turkey guns would be complete without at least some mention of front-end loaders. Whether it's from traditionalists, tinkerers, or merely those seeking a change of pace, there has been increasing interest in muzzleloading shotguns for turkeys. Available models range from authentic antiques and replicas to modern versions with in-line ignition systems. Most come with simple bead sights, though newer ones and in-lines typically have fiber-optic sights.

The major difference between muzzleloaders and modern-day shotguns is

■ Advancements in modern muzzleloaders have prompted many turkey hunters to take up the added challenge of hunting with a smokepole.

that rather than an enclosed shotshell, the components of your loads will be powder, shot, shot cup wad, and overshot wad. (The hunter's nickname for these primitive-style weapons is "smokepole." You can understand why!) For powder use black powder or any of its modern substitutes. Never use smokeless powder. Your owner's manual should give recommended powder-charge sizes. If it doesn't, you should be using something in the neighborhood of 90 to 100 grains. Also, pellets are not recommended for muzzle-loading shotguns; stick to loose powder. For shot, use chilled lead shot, available wherever shotgun-reloading supplies are sold. You can use standard shotgun wads, but those designed for muzzleloaders will hold twice the amount of shot used in a standard 2¾-inch shotshell. The last component, the overshot wad, will hold the shot in place.

You have several choices in ignition systems. Flintlocks are not available on most newer guns, and they're prone to misfire. Still, they may be preferred by the black-powder purist. Most modern muzzleloading shotguns are equipped with a caplock ignition system, including side-hammer and in-line types. Some of the newer in-lines are ignited by a 209 shotgun primer. The latter is the most reliable type, as it seals the nipple, preventing any moisture from reaching the powder.

Along with shot components, you'll need the usual possibles (a mountain-man term for miscellaneous accessories): a nipple or breech-plug wrench and nipple pick for in-the-field cleaning between shots or in the event of a misfire. You can speed up your reloading time by carrying premeasured powder and shot charges in airtight "speed-loader" capsules and, if you use a capping tool, preloaded with caps.

Patterning your muzzleloader is more important and involved but offers several advantages. First, you're not restricted by fixed loads. Because you can vary both shot and powder in small increments, you can tinker until you find just the right combination. Also, because you can buy both in bulk, patterning is less expensive than with a modern shotgun.

## Conclusion

Whatever gun-load combination you ultimately choose, the most important thing is that you use a gun you are both comfortable with and familiar with. If you're comfortable with it, you'll shoot better, regardless of its physical parameters. And if you're familiar with it, you'll know what it's capable of, how far you can shoot, where to aim, and when to pass up a shot. If you use the same gun over several seasons, all these things eventually become instinctive. You and your gun become one.

# CHAPTER THREE

# Gobbler Gear

**N**atural selection is a process wherein only those individuals best equipped to deal with the conditions at hand will be successful. In the natural world of tooth and claw, success means remaining alive long enough to pass along your genes—survival of the fittest. Turkey hunting is not so much a life-and-death struggle, at least not for the hunter. In both cases, though, the real test of "equipment" only occurs during extremes.

It's kind of like optics. Under average conditions most hunters would never recognize or appreciate the difference between $100 binoculars and $1,000 binoculars. But in the first and last thirty minutes of shooting light, the high-end optics are worth every extra penny you spent on them.

The same is true for much of your other turkey-hunting gear. Some of it may seem unnecessary, until you encounter extreme conditions. I never expect to hunt in the snow but can't count on one hand the number of times I've stepped off a plane somewhere in April, only to be greeted by bone-chilling cold and wind-driven snow. You hope it doesn't rain, but if it does, are you going to squander your valuable

hunting time back at camp watching the Outdoor Channel? Or are you gonna go out and brave the storm?

Comfort is key. It keeps you in the woods. Comfort means being cool when it's hot, warm when it's cold, and dry when it's wet. It means no backaches, no blisters, and no bug bites.

Beyond that, there are many gear choices that can make you more successful. We'll try to cover the gamut, illustrating the latest and greatest.

## Apparel

What you wear or what you don't wear is the number-one factor in keeping you comfortable. And one of the first keys is to dress in layers. You can always take one off if you don't need it. But you can't put one on if you don't have it.

I may be the exception (though I doubt it), but I rarely hunt without a base layer, regardless of conditions. That layer usually consists of some type of synthetic material that breathes well and wicks away perspiration. You can vary the thickness according to temperature.

Turkeys don't care if you smell, but you and your hunting companions might. It's no problem if there's a washing machine handy. It could be a problem, though, if you're in a remote camp for a week with only one or two shirts.

The next layer can vary considerably with conditions. If it's really cold, you may want a middle or insulating layer of polar fleece, which has the same breathable, moisture-control (and antimicrobial) properties as your base layer. Otherwise, you can go straight to your outer layer. Cotton is a good option in cool, dry conditions but will be too warm if it's hot and useless if you get wet. A better option for hotter temperatures or warm, wet days is a lightweight synthetic material like Trek-Lite. If it's cool, add a fleece sweatshirt. If it's really cold, you may opt for a Thinsulate-lined coat. If the forecast calls for rain, wear pants and a jacket lined with Gore-Tex or some other waterproof breathable laminate.

Another consideration, particularly with regard to pants, is durability. Turkeys seem to favor areas with lots of thorns and sometimes barbed wire, and you'll need something that is tear resistant and tough. That's why denim is better than plain cotton.

Another option well worth considering is a three-dimensional outer layer or so-called leafy suit. Military snipers have

■ So-called snake or turkey boots provide the best all-around footwear for the spring turkey hunter, offering a durable exterior, good ankle support, and a rugged sole for rough terrain. Waterproof models round out your footwear needs.

Good moisture-wicking base layers have been around for a while. A recent innovation is material treated with antimicrobial odor-suppressing technology.

used them for years, but when they first came on the market as hunting apparel, many hunters, myself included, were skeptical. That changed the first time I wore one. Birds even a few feet away virtually ignored me. Now it's almost standard wear for me, particularly when I'm bowhunting.

## Footwear

Obviously, you'll need a pair of boots, and your two primary concerns should be comfort and concealment. I've tried just about every type of footwear imaginable and found that the best all-around choice for turkey hunting is the so-called snake boot or turkey boot. Its Cordura and leather uppers will stand up to any terrain and outlast other materials, such as rubber or neoprene. The turkey boot offers more ankle and arch support than most other styles. Add a Gore-Tex liner, and it's waterproof, yet still breathable. And yes, it does protect you from snakes.

As with guns, camouflage finish isn't necessary but is worthy of strong consideration. Anything that helps you blend better into your surroundings is an asset. At the very least, you need a pair of dark-colored boots with no shiny buckles, clips, or grommets. Sunlight reflecting off anything shiny could be enough to give away your presence.

■ Which camo pattern you choose isn't critical; however, you should try to match the habitat and time of the season you'll be hunting in. Darker colors with more brown and gray are better for early-season hunting, while those with more green are better later in the spring. The reverse is true in the fall.

Footwear also includes socks. Remember the motto: Cotton is rotten. Cotton absorbs and retains moisture, leaving you with wet (and sometimes cold) feet, which will blister more easily. A better choice is a thin polypropylene or acrylic sock liner with a Thermax, wool, or wool-blend sock—lighter when it's warm and heavier when it's cool. Combining this system with a Gore-Tex boot will wick moisture away from your feet, keeping them dry and comfortable.

### Headwear

You have several options to choose from regarding hats. Obviously, camouflage is a requirement. A visor is helpful to shade your eyes from the sun. However, a full brim can block sound. That's why I prefer a baseball-cap style. A mesh back is better for warm conditions and a solid back for cooler days. A camo wool or fleece cap offers more comfort on cold mornings, and of course, wear Gore-Tex on rainy days.

### Other

A couple of other accessories you'll need are a head net and gloves. Both should be camo or at least drab in color. I usually lose a couple of pairs of gloves over the course of the season, so I keep a good supply on hand and always carry at least one extra pair afield. Cotton gloves are fine, and if you want to save money you can pick up

■ The number-one killer in the outdoors is hypothermia from exposure. That's why it's so important to have good clothes that will keep you dry and warm. Besides, when it rains, the turkeys are still out there, and you should be, too.

brown Jersey gloves at most hardware stores for a few dollars a pair.

The type of head net you use will depend largely on personal preference. I prefer a cooler, ventilated mesh material over solid cotton. I also prefer a three-quarter mask rather than a full hood, as I can pull it down and wear it loosely around my neck when I'm not working a bird. Finally, I prefer a mask with a wire rim around the eyes. This allows me to shape the mask opening tight to my eyes, whereas more loosely fitting masks will sometimes obscure my peripheral vision.

As you can see, clothing is a key ingredient in the recipe for turkey-hunting success. You need something that will keep you dry when it's wet and warm when it's cold, will protect you against thorns and bugs, and will conceal you from the turkey's keen vision. The more comfortable you are and the more functional your clothing, the better, longer, and harder you'll hunt. And your hunt will be more enjoyable.

## Accessories

An entire chapter could be written on the contents of your vest: what you should or could carry and, more important, why. What you really need can vary with circumstances and personal preference. You might not carry as much for a quick morning hunt as you would if you were out for the day. Some folks take the Boy Scout motto of "Be prepared" seriously, while others are content to make do with what they have.

The following are some suggestions for what I consider the essential items your turkey vest should contain, with some options for various circumstances and conditions. As you spend more time afield, you can add or subtract from the list to suit your individual needs and hunting style.

Obviously, you'll be taking calls. They're the single most important item you'll carry in your vest, but because we'll cover them more extensively in the next chapter, we'll skip over calls for now. I will, however, mention a call-care kit. Most friction calls require some maintenance as you use them. You'll need chalk for your box calls and small patches of sandpaper and scrub pads for your slates. All of this will fit neatly into a snuff can or even a film canister. Several companies make call tools, some about the size of a toothbrush, with faces of various abrasive materials for roughing up your slates.

The vast majority of turkey hunts begin well before daylight, which requires a source of artificial light to find our way into the woods—a flashlight. As a general rule, the smaller, the better. You'll only use it for a short time, but you will have to carry it all day. The most commonly used light among turkey hunters is the Mini-Mag style, which runs on two AA batteries. Some of the newer ones have more powerful LED lights and sometimes have options for low and high power. An even better option is

■ While not everything you carry with you may be necessary, the more "stuff" you tote the more options you'll have. Pictured here are all of the items I carry afield with me.

a headlamp, which frees up your hands to carry your gun and fend away branches.

One of the most overlooked pieces of gear is also one of the most important. You should consider a compass an absolute necessity. Before you head into the woods, take a bearing on the road and your intended direction of travel. You can also take bearings throughout the day to keep track of where you're going and which is the quickest way out. If you should wound a bird, you can take a bearing on which way it went, as wounded turkeys will often travel in a straight line.

A handheld GPS unit can often be even more useful but should always be considered secondary to a compass (after all, the batteries will never go dead in your compass). Take the GPS when scouting, then use it to find your way back to the hotspots. Keep it on as you hunt, then look for the shortest, most direct route back to the truck when you're done. Some units even allow you to download topo maps and aerial photos (two more items worth carrying in your vest) directly into the unit.

I typically carry a couple of hand tools with me. A multipurpose tool is handy for fashioning decoy stakes, dislodging jammed shells, adjusting box calls, and more. The other item I carry is a hand pruner. It adds extra weight, but the number of times I need one on any given day more than compensates for the weight. It always seems like there are one or two branches obscuring my view, blocking the swing of my gun barrel, or jabbing me in the back. A hand pruner makes quick work of them.

Number one in the personal-comfort-and-safety department is a small water bottle. On warm, dry days you'll find it's well worth carrying the extra weight, and should you get lost, it could mean survival. It can also help wet your whistle if you get so nerved up you can't work your mouth call.

A light snack will help reenergize you and stave off hunger. Energy bars and dried fruit are great ideas. I prefer bite-size candy bars, though I often end up with some funky-looking junk in the bottom of my pockets by season's end.

Another essential, at least for me, is toilet tissue. No need to expound on that. I will add, though, that keeping it in a ziplock bag instead of your pocket helps it last longer. If you're really into comfort, consider moist wipes as an alternative. And be sure to bury your, um, evidence. Enough said about that.

Regardless of whether I hunt on public land or private land, I typically carry an orange vest or cap. After killing a bird, or sometimes merely when moving from one location to another, I'll don the orange, making myself more visible to other hunters. This is a matter of both safety and consideration. You won't be mistaken as game, and other hunters will be able to detect your presence from a long distance away. Most turkey vests now come with orange

■ The older I get the more difficult it is for me to remain comfortable while sitting for long periods of time. I don't mind admitting that I consider a padded seat cushion a necessity.

flags that can be stowed in zippered pockets until needed.

The next group of items includes often-overlooked essentials and their accessories. You wouldn't forget your shells, right? I have, and if you hunt long enough, so will you. It makes for a very short hunt.

How about licenses and tags? On just about every hunt I've ever been on, at some point someone leaves these back at camp. That's a definite no-no. Not only is it an inconvenience, but it could get you into trouble. It's also a good idea to carry a small pen or pencil for filling out your tag

and an electrical zip tie or cable tie to affix it to your bird.

What's the number-one lost or misplaced item among turkey hunters? It's probably close to a tie between a face mask and a pair of camo gloves. That's why I always carry a spare of both items in my vest. They weigh next to nothing and take up almost no space, but having a spare of either could save your hunt or your companion's.

Though they're certainly not a necessity, I rarely hunt without decoys. I'll discuss the whys and hows in a later chapter.

■ Decoys offer many advantages. How and when you use them and how many you use will vary according to each situation.

For now, let it suffice to say that they're well worth considering, and you have a ton of options to choose from. If weight is a factor, go light. But if you'll be sitting in a blind all morning, not far off the road, you can use more and heavier models. Incidentally, it doesn't hurt to carry an extra stake or two in case you lose or break one.

## The Vest

Then, of course, you'll need something to put all this junk in; you have lots of options here as well. If you carry a lot of stuff, you need a lot of pockets to keep individual items sorted and easy to find. There's seemingly no limit to the variety of options with regard to pocket size, configuration, location, and means of fastening. You'll just have to shop around and see what best suits you. Some vests are small and light and have only a few pockets. Others are larger, with many pockets, for pack rats like myself.

In any case you'll very likely spend a good deal of time sitting, and the ground

### BEATING THE BUGS

One of the biggest nuisances of turkey hunting is bugs: blackflies, mosquitoes, chiggers and ticks. Fortunately, there are ways to beat them, both mechanically and chemically.

One option is a bug-proof mesh suit. These work well but they can be costly. I find that the head net obscures my vision. Another mechanical deterrent is a bite-proof base layer such as Rhinoskin, which is particularly effective against ticks and chiggers. On the chemical side you have several choices of repellents. Recent studies have clearly demonstrated that DEET-based repellents are the most effective against mosquitoes and blackflies and are not harmful to humans. However, they wear off over time. Duranon, permethrin, and similar products are more effective against ticks and chiggers. They are applied to your clothing rather than your body and will remain effective for several weeks.

A more recent innovation is the ThermaCELL (pictured). It's a device with a tiny heating element and a pad saturated with repellent. It adds a little more bulk and weight to your vest, but all things considered, it is the most efficient and effective mosquito repellent available.

can be cold, wet, and uncomfortable. I strongly recommend a vest with a padded seat attached. Some vests even come with rigid internal frames or webbed straps to help support your back, a real plus when good cover is scarce.

## Conclusion

Perhaps the best advice I can give about your turkey-hunting gear is to not worry too much about getting it right the first time. Often there is no one right item; several different types or styles might work equally well. One might be better suited to a specific set of circumstances one day but not applicable at all the next or under different circumstances.

That's fine, because turkey hunting is a progression. Or as my friend Jim Casada likes to say, "In the school of the outdoors, graduation day never arrives." Furthermore, turkey hunters are gadget junkies, worse even than deer hunters. We're constantly seeking something better or simply something new to add to our toolbox.

There are two types of outdoorsmen in the turkey woods: turkey hunters and those who hunt turkeys. If your pupils dilate and your pulse quickens every time you walk into an outdoor shop and see camo on the racks and turkey calls on the shelf, you're a turkey hunter. If you buy several new calls every year, whether you need them or not, you're a turkey hunter. If you're just never satisfied with your outfit, you're a turkey hunter.

# CHAPTER FOUR

# Turkey Calling

For all the emphasis it receives, you'd think that calling is an absolute necessity to successful turkey hunting. It's not. You can kill a turkey without ever making a sound—and I've done so on more than one occasion. Like your other equipment, however, when it really counts, it can make a huge difference. And the more proficient you are at calling, the more successful you'll be at hunting. Proficiency involves knowing not only what to say but when to say it. It's a bit like learning a foreign language: You're literally learning how to talk turkey.

■ Calling, for the most part, consists of imitating hens to attract gobblers in the spring and either-sex birds in the fall.

The goal of this chapter, though, is not to teach you fluent turkey. If you were going on a vacation to Paris, you couldn't learn French by one reading of a single chapter. Likewise, there aren't enough pages in this book to teach you all there is to know about turkey calling. There is

■ Turkey hunters once relied primarily on woods-manship and stealth, but calling has become the basis for modern spring turkey hunting.

space enough to teach you basic, conversational turkey. The rest you can pick up along the way—in actual conversation.

Before we begin vocabulary lessons, we need to understand the message we are trying to convey. In simple terms we're saying, "I'm a turkey, and I'm over here. Come on over and join me." In spring the message is a bit more specific. It's mating season, and you're inviting a male bird by imitating a female. In effect you're saying, "Hey, big boy, let's get it on."

Numerous sources, written and otherwise, will tell you that this is nigh onto impossible because it's unnatural. "In the natural world," they say, "it's the tom who calls the hen to him. Trying to call him to a hen makes the tom go against his natural disposition." The fact of the matter is that gobblers will, and quite often do, move toward calling they perceive to be a real hen—sometimes quite willingly and aggressively. If they didn't, we wouldn't kill nearly as many as we do. You just need to say the right words.

## Calls: Components of the Turkey's Vocabulary

According to some sources, the turkey's vocabulary consists of as many as thirty distinct calls. Fortunately, to hunt them you'll really only ever need to know about a half-dozen. Like a good foreign-language program, we'll start with the basics and work up.

## The Yelp

I contend that the "yelp" is the foundation of all turkey calling. It is the call most used by turkeys and is the basis for most other turkey vocalizations. It is also the call most familiar to hunters, the easiest to mimic, and the one most often utilized—in one form or another—to lure a bird.

The basic yelp is a two-note call, beginning with a high-pitched *kee* and ending with a lower-pitched *yuk*, typically described as a *kee-yuk* or *kee-yawk* sound. To the normal ear the *kee* and the *yuk* are blended together to sound like a single note, sometimes described as *chalk*. However, knowing that it is actually a two-note call is important in learning how to imitate it.

With friction calls you start by exerting more pressure on your striker or paddle to get the *kee*, then ease up to get the *yuk*. Similarly, with diaphragms you press harder with your tongue to get the *kee*, then lower your tongue and drop your jaw to get the *yuk*. Practice till you get your *kee-yuk* right, then speed it up until it sounds more like a single-syllable *kyuk*. That's the yelp.

The "plain yelp" is the most commonly used version of this call. A typical rendition consists of repeating the yelp five to seven times. If you can do this, you can kill a turkey—sometimes.

The exact meaning varies with time and place. Sometimes it's simply a hen announcing her presence: "I'm a turkey, and I'm over here." In the spring it's also a way for her to attract a mate. "Hey, big guy, why don't you come on over here?"

The "tree yelp" is a muted, softer version, usually repeated only three or four times. As its name implies, it's a sound turkeys make on the roost, typically as they first begin to stir in the morning, before fly-down. To imitate it, emphasize the *yuk* part of your yelp, and do it as softly and quietly as you can. This call is best used before fly-down, to dupe a randy gobbler into thinking there are hens roosted nearby.

The "assembly yelp" is similar to the plain yelp, only a bit more insistent and often longer—using more notes. It's employed by the hen to gather or assemble her brood flock. Thus, it's most often used in fall hunting. She's saying, "C'mon, guys and gals, let's gather up. It's time to move on."

The same is true for the "lost yelp." It is slightly louder and lower in pitch than the plain yelp and may be repeated as many as thirty times. Turkeys are gregarious creatures, particularly in the fall, and when they get separated, they get anxious. It's as if they're saying, "Hey, is there anybody out there? Anybody at all? Hello! Somebody?"

## The Cluck

Sometimes the yelp is sped up to the point where the *kee* is virtually indistinguishable, leaving only the *yuk*, or "cluck"—a short, sharp note that sounds just like its name. This cluck is used by turkeys, and turkey hunters, in a variety of ways, alone or in conjunction with other calls. It's made on friction calls by either picking the surface of your slate with a peg or striking your box sharply with the paddle. With a diaphragm, simply mouth the word *cut*, *tut*, or *hut*.

You may hear a hen uttering single clucks at spaced-out intervals as she feeds contentedly along. It's also been suggested that turkeys use the cluck as a way for flock members to keep track of one another in thick cover. Again, we don't know the actual meaning for sure, but we do know that by imitating the cluck, in its various configurations, you can make a turkey come closer to you. Some hunters will throw a few stray clucks in with their yelping to "dress" their calling. The cluck is also often used along with the purr (see below) to create a cluck-and-purr.

## Cutting

Stringing together multiple, more-excited clucks in rapid succession is called "cutting." This call may signal excitement or aggression. When he's in the right mood, you can really fire up a gobbler by cutting at him. However, this call is easy to overuse, so err on the side of caution. Use it sparingly and conservatively unless you feel confident your aggressive calling is doing the trick.

You also need to be careful because the cutt sounds similar to another call that has an entirely different meaning. When a turkey sees or senses danger, it sounds

an alarm "putt." This sounds very much like the cluck, except it is typically sharper and louder and is often repeated numerous times in rapid succession. It also has a ventriloquial quality, making it difficult to determine the direction of origin. To the turkey it means danger. To the hunter it means the game is over. If you have a shot, take it now or forever hold your fire.

Another variation of cutting is the "cackle"—some combination of excited cutts and yelps. The version most often used by turkeys and hunters alike is the fly-down cackle, designed to mimic a turkey as it leaves the roost. It starts out with short, rapid cutts, then tapers to longer, more drawn-out cutts as the bird nears the ground, sometimes ending in a few plain yelps when it hits the ground.

The third variation—the "purr"— might best be described as a tree yelp with a rattle or roll. It sounds like its name and is also a contented feeding call. As mentioned above, it is often combined with a cluck, to produce the cluck-and-purr (or purr-and-cluck). On friction calls you make it by drawing the peg across the slate or the paddle across the box slowly. On a diaphragm you simply purr with your tongue while slowly exhaling.

The purr has its own variation, called the "fighting purr" or "rattle." It's merely a louder, more aggressive, and prolonged version. Like antler rattling in whitetails, it's a sound toms or jakes make when sparring, and it sometimes works similarly to attract other males. You might frighten off

■ To make your calling more effective, you need to take a bird's "temperature"—see how he reacts to your initial calls, then adjust accordingly.

more birds than you call, though, so use this one sparingly.

## Kee-Kee

To this point we've addressed mostly the "*yuk*" half of the yelp. The first half, or *kee*, is also used alone, to make the *kee-kee*. Predominantly a fall call, it consists of several short, high-pitched whistling notes and is used by young birds that have not quite developed their voices. Poults may *kee-kee* any time, but they become particularly vocal when separated from their flock.

As the young birds become older and more vocally adept, they may break from the high-pitched *kee-kee*s into yelps. This is called a "*kee-kee* run." It's kind of like a teenage boy whose voice cracks as he's going through puberty. Though used predominantly in the fall, spring hunters will sometimes use the *kee-kee* to make a strutting or moving tom stop and stick his neck up, making him a better target.

## Yelpless

There are a couple of calls worth noting that are not variations of the yelp and that, unlike the others, are male-only calls. One in particular is the gobble. It's the sound that stirs the soul of every turkey hunter and makes our hearts pound, our pulses quicken, and our mouths go dry. This is the mating call of the male turkey. It's used primarily to attract hens, though toms will often gobble in response to a loud noise.

When hunting public land, or anywhere other hunters are present, this call is a no-no. You might sound enough like a real tom to possibly put yourself in harm's way. If you're certain you're alone, though, it can be effective. To a tom it may represent a challenge from a rival male.

Another male-only call is the "spit-and-drum," also sometimes called the "chump and hum." This two-part call is not a vocalization. The "spit" is a sharp exhalation of air—like a sneeze. This is followed by a very soft, deep, bassy sound the gobbler makes by resonating air in his chest. Gobblers only make this sound while strutting. Furthermore, it's a short-range sound. If you hear it, you'd better be ready because the bird is close—real close.

## Miscellaneous

There are several other types of sounds you may hear and can use during the course of your hunt. One is the "locator call." As previously mentioned, toms will sometimes "shock gobble" in response to a loud noise. If you can make him do that, you know where he is; and if you can do it without sounding like a turkey, his attention won't be focused on you.

The most common locator call is the barred owl call, often used to locate a roosted tom the night before or on the morning of a hunt. To imitate it you give several successive hoots in a pneumonic cadence that goes: "who cooks for you; who cooks for you all." If you can't do it with your voice, several commercial owl calls are available.

A coyote howl will sometimes serve the same purpose and may even work better in heavily hunted areas. After a while, turkeys become conditioned to owl calling and won't respond as readily. But if you hit 'em with the coyote howl, it may startle them because it's something they don't hear as often.

You can also use locator calls throughout the day. If things are slow, you may want to try shocking a bird with a crow, peacock, coyote, or woodpecker call. A standard "caw, caw" might shock a bird, but they hear crows cawing all day. It's often more effective to sound like a very excited crow.

A much more specialized sound is the wing flap. As turkeys fly down from the roost, their big wings make a ton of noise and often slap against branches. You can make the same sound with a hat or a real turkey wing secured from a previous kill. Just slap it against a tree as you are doing your fly-down cackle to add a bit of realism to your calling sequence.

One last sound worth mentioning is a subtle but sometimes deadly effective turkey call. The rustle of leaves is almost a constant background noise associated with turkeys in the forest; the birds are seemingly always in motion, and as they travel along they turn over leaves searching for edible morsels hidden underneath. Adding this background noise to your calling can sometimes tip the balance on a reluctant tom. And on particularly wary gobblers, it's sometimes more effective when used without any calling.

## Practical Application

Now that you are familiar with the vocabulary, we need to work on composition. For that we'll invent some theoretical hunting situations and offer some suggestions on how to converse with your quarry.

### Lesson 1: The Roost

It's the evening before the hunt, and we're out trying to locate turkeys. We get to a location where we think birds are present. We wait until just before or just after the sun sets, then we give our barred owl hoot: "who-cooks-for-you; who-cooks-for-yoooo-all." If a bird answers, we're all set. If not, try a few more times. Still no answer? Get out your coyote howler, and give it a loud blast. There! It was a long way off, but it was definitely a gobble. We're all set for tomorrow morning.

### Lesson 2: Daybreak Calling

After a restless night's sleep, you woke well before dawn, sneaked within calling distance of your roosted bird, and set up.

Now the eastern sky is turning a pinkish gray, and from the roost come the first gobbles of dawn.

A typical serenade, if there is such a thing, might go something like this: Begin with a few soft tree yelps, imitating a hen just waking and stirring on the roost. This alerts the gobbler to your presence and location. No matter how much he gobbles, do nothing more until shooting light arrives.

When it does, start with a few clucks and maybe some softer yelping. Hopefully, he'll respond. If he does, increase the intensity a little, as if you're a nervous hen preparing to fly down. Then let him have it with both barrels: Hit him with a fly-down cackle accompanied by some wing flapping. Finish off with some yelping or cutting, and get ready. The game is on.

### Lesson 3: Keep the Conversation Going

You've initiated the conversation, and the bird has responded. What happens next, and for the rest of your hunt, will depend largely on how the tom reacts to your continued calling and how you then respond. You want to keep the bird interested without intimidating him.

Unfortunately, there aren't too many hard and fast rules. When it comes to calling, the biggest mistake turkey hunters make is calling too much. But the second-biggest mistake is not calling enough. The trick is finding the middle ground and determining what the right

■ Every encounter with a gobbler is unique. The same gobbler may react differently to different calls on different days or even at different times on the same day. That's why you need to be able to interpret his response and react accordingly.

amount is in terms of volume, frequency, and intensity.

Solving that riddle isn't made any easier by the fact that turkeys can be extremely fickle. One day a tom will trip over his beard running to your position, and you could call him by swinging a rusty gate. The next day that same bird may seem totally indifferent to your calling.

That's when knowing what to say can tip the balance in your favor, and that knowledge will only come with experience. You've got to feel the bird out, take his temperature, mix and match. If he's clearly not responding, back off. Give a few soft calls occasionally to remind him you're there, but let him do his thing. Or

move on to another bird. If he gobbles but seems indifferent, continue calling but maybe ease up a bit. If he gobbles aggressively to your every call, keep calling; maybe even crank it up a notch. Once you're certain he's on his way, you can taper off or stop calling. He knows exactly where you are—no need to overcall and scare him off now.

## Conclusion

These are gross generalizations, but they should get you through many of the more typical situations and provide a foundation upon which to build your communication skills. Speaking fluent turkey takes time and lots of practice. You can learn from other, more experienced hunters, but the best teachers are the ones you pursue with gun or bow.

# CHAPTER FIVE

# Scouting

I was racing down Interstate 295, on my way to an out-of-state hunt and going much too fast, when I saw the unmarked Mustang parked in the median . . . too late. In my rearview mirror I saw the car pull onto the highway and the blue lights go on. I knew he had me, but I held out one last hope that maybe it was just coincidence—perhaps he was chasing someone else, or there was an accident farther south. No such luck. He pulled up behind me, and I knew I was done for.

It was a generic state trooper's face that greeted me at the window, shaded by a wide-brimmed cap, eyes hidden behind mirrored sunglasses. He was cordial enough as he advised me the reason for the stop: "72 in a 55." I hung my head and contritely handed him my license and registration.

He turned and started back toward his vehicle, then stopped. "Uh-oh." Thoughts raced through my head. *Did I forget to renew my driver's license? Had the registration expired?* His next question took me so much by surprise that I was speechless. "Did you go to Hamilton-Wenham Regional High?" Was this some sort of

■ **The more time you spend scouting, the less time you'll need to spend hunting.**

trick question? How did he figure that out so fast? I looked first at his face as he lowered the "man with no eyes" glasses, then at his name tag, and suddenly it clicked—an old high school chum.

Things suddenly took a much better turn as we shared the usual "what ya been up to" cordialities. They improved even more when he asked where I was headed. "Why are you going out of state to hunt turkeys?" he responded. "They're out behind my house every morning."

I decided to go for broke. "I'll be back in a week; do you suppose I could come by and, uh, give your place a try?" The one-word answer, "anytime," was all I needed to hear. Bingo! New turkey-hunting spot.

That one worked pretty well for me. I even took a client in there the following week and called his first bird to the gun. But I wouldn't want to depend on that kind of good fortune for all my turkey-hunting spots.

The truth of the matter is that I spend a considerable amount of time looking for good hunting grounds. Many factors contribute to a successful hunt, but scouting stands head and shoulders above the rest. In fact, there's an inverse correlation: The more time you spend scouting, the less time you'll spend hunting. And while I enjoy the process, my ultimate goal is to succeed.

## Locating Birds

Obviously, before you can hunt birds you've got to find them. When I started hunting turkeys twenty-five years ago, that was one of the most difficult aspects. In most of the country, that's no longer the case. I daresay that in most states turkeys at least occupy, if not proliferate in, most areas of favorable habitat. The greater challenge nowadays is finding birds where you can hunt them. We'll get into how to locate them on a broad scale in a subsequent chapter. For now we'll restrict our discussion to a more localized level.

## Word of Mouth

It's no secret what my favorite spring activity is. My neighbors know it, and so do the mailman, the UPS and FedEx drivers, the local sheriff, and at least one state trooper. They love to talk about turkeys and where they've seen them. I enjoy listening even more, and these folks are among my best sources for new locations. However, they're hardly my only source.

## Windshield Scouting

Wherever and whenever I'm in a vehicle, I'm always watching for deer and turkeys and taking mental notes when I see them (I wish I was more conscientious about actually writing the stuff down). I also spend a considerable amount of time purposely looking for them and have learned several tactics that have helped me become much more efficient in my efforts.

Timing is a big factor. While I may do some preliminary scouting in late winter, I usually wait until the breeding season begins before I devote any serious

■ It's important that you know what to look for and know how to interpret what you find.

effort. As winter flocks disband, they may relocate—sometimes to considerable distances—before the hunting season. The closer you get to hunting season, the more valuable your scouting missions.

Time of day is also important, and the best advice I can offer is to scout at the same time of day when you'll hunt. Casual hunters go when it's convenient, which may be midmorning or midafternoon. That's okay if you plan on hunting those

hours. But birds can cover a lot of ground in a few hours and could already be miles from where they roost.

These casual hunters also do most of their scouting from the road. This takes considerably less effort but has some distinct disadvantages. First and foremost, if you can see turkeys from the road, so can everyone else. These birds become famous with the locals, and you can almost bet there will be a crowd at that spot on

# Signs for Locating Wild Turkeys

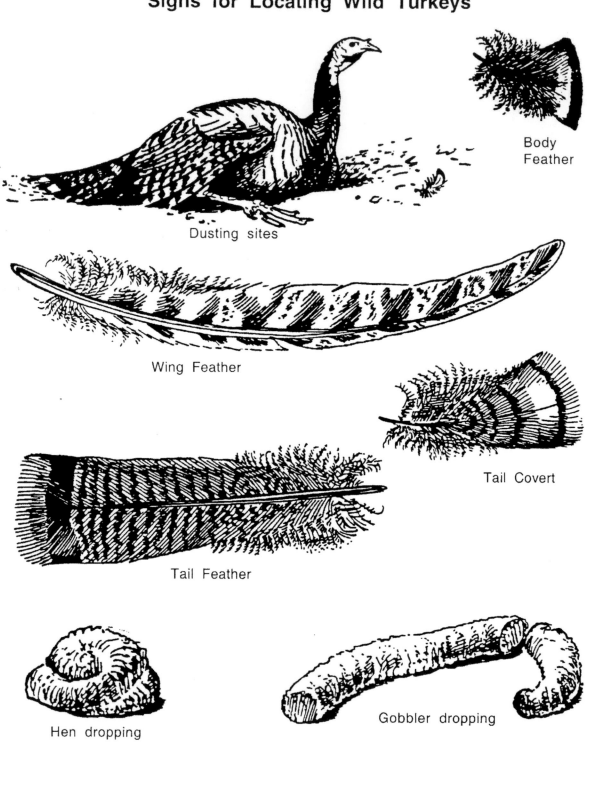

Body
Feather

Dusting sites

Wing Feather

Tail Covert

Tail Feather

Hen dropping

Gobbler dropping

■ Feathers, scat, and dusting bowls are just some of the sign you should be looking for when
scouting. COURTESY OF THE NATIONAL WILD TURKEY FEDERATION

opening day. Another disadvantage is that you're only seeing a fraction of the birds in the area.

A lot more folks scout later in the afternoon, after work. That's okay, too, as it will give you a rough idea where the birds are going to roost. The best time, however, is at dawn.

## From a Distance

You can cover far more ground if you scout not only by sight but also by sound. For me a typical scouting mission begins about forty-five minutes before sunrise. I start by driving the local roads, stopping every quarter-mile or so to get out and listen for gobbling. On still mornings, and in the right terrain, the sound will carry for over a mile. This allows me to scout vast areas with minimal effort. Sometimes I'll hear a bird but can't pinpoint its location. That's when I get a bit more technical.

If I want a more precise location on a distant gobbler, I do what's known as triangulation. I use a topo map, a pencil, and a compass, though a GPS is mighty helpful, too. Upon locating a gobbling bird, I use my compass to take a bearing on the bird. Next, I draw a pencil line on the map from my position to where I think the gobbler is. I move to another location and do this again. Once I've done this from three different locations, the intersection of the three lines identifies the gobbler's position.

Bear in mind that turkeys don't always roost in the same spot. A bird could move from one site to another, and a new bird could show up overnight. That's why it's to your advantage to do your scouting as often as possible, increasing your frequency as hunting season draws nearer.

## The Buddy System

Another way you can reduce your scouting time is by sharing the load. I hunt with friends from in town, out of town, and out of state. We each have particular areas we're responsible for. I cover my ground; they cover theirs. When we hunt together, we act as guides for one another.

## Read the Signs

I used to spend considerably more time scouting for sign than I have in recent years. However, I still find sign-scouting treks valuable, particularly when I'm hunting a new area or scouting during the middle of the day when birds are quiet. You can also learn certain things from sign that you can't from merely seeing or hearing birds.

The most abundant and easily recognized sign is scratching. As turkeys travel along the forest floor, they scratch away leaves and duff to uncover food. In doing so, they leave patches of bare ground, much like a deer pawing for acorns. Turkeys are much less delicate feeders than deer, and they'll scratch up big patches of leaves. Large areas of turned-over leaves may indicate a lot of birds or regular use.

Either way, it's a good sign—it tells you they've been feeding in the area. But when? Look more closely at the leaves and the ground to determine how fresh the sign is. Are the undersides of the overturned leaves or the bare ground still moist? Or is the ground dried out? Look also for new shoots in the bare earth, evidence the scratching may be older.

You can also tell which way the birds were traveling. As they feed, they usually travel in a more or less linear direction. When they scratch, they pull away the leaves in front of them and pile them in back.

Feeding is not the only activity that leaves evidence of turkey use. Every evening turkeys fly to roost in large trees, often routinely using the same grove or even the same trees. As they sit and preen, they'll drop feathers and poop. An accumulation of either, or both, is a good indication you've located a roost. Turkeys tend to prefer roosting in softwoods, when available, and you may also find a lot of small broken twigs on the ground under a roost.

There won't always be evidence of scratching on the ground, but you can look for other signs, such as droppings. Turkeys leave black and white droppings that look much the same as any bird dropping, except larger. You can even distinguish the sex of the bird that left its calling card.

Those of a hen are spiraled and bulbous, and look almost like a kernel of popped corn. The gobbler's are elongated and "L" or "J" shaped; just remember: "J" for jake. Identifying the sex of the dropping maker is less important in the spring because where there are hens, there will be toms. That's not always the case in the fall.

You can also look for signs of courtship activity. While the hens feed, toms spend a considerable amount of time strutting. A

■ Turkeys leave black and white droppings. Those of a hen are spiraled and bulbous and look almost like a kernel of popped corn.

■ The gobbler's droppings are elongated and "L" or "J" shaped. There are, however, exceptions in every case.

tom in full strut will lower his wings and drag the tips along the ground. In soft, loose soil, these drag marks are very obvious and indicate a prime spot to lay an ambush.

A similarly useful sign, and one that's often overlooked, is a dusting site. It consists of little more than a concave bowl of exposed soil, formed when turkeys "bathe" in the dusty soil, presumably to rid themselves of parasites such as feather lice. These bowls are somewhat analogous to deer scrapes—although used for bathing rather than courtship. They are visited regularly and can be especially productive later in the morning, after turkeys are done feeding.

## Watch 'Em

So we've found some huntable birds. We know where they feed, and we know where they roost. We should be all set, right? Wrong!

This is where so many hunters mess up. They locate a bird or birds, sneak in under cover of darkness, set out their decoys, and wait. Dawn arrives, they hear gobbling, and they begin calling. A bird seems to be responding. The woods grow lighter. They hear the sound of flapping wings, followed by more gobbling. Instead of coming toward them, though, the sounds are moving farther away.

I've been guilty of that myself. Sometimes we have no choice; for instance, if we're hunting new ground. If at all possible, however, you should spend time with your birds before you hunt them. Find out not only where they roost but which way they fly down, where they touch down, and where they go from there. In short, learn their routine.

## Roosting

I've saved this technique for last, partly because that's when it should be used. Roosting is a technique for locating birds the night before your hunt. You simply go to a prospective hunting area at or slightly after dusk and make a loud noise—usually by imitating the calls of barred owls or coyotes. Turkeys will often react to any loud noise by shock gobbling, thus giving away their location.

The reason you should wait until the eve of your hunt to do this is that birds can become conditioned to shock calls. If you or some other hunter does this every night for a week, eventually the birds won't gobble anymore. Or if you're the third or fourth guy to shock the roost in the same night, you may not get an answer.

Bear in mind also that sometimes toms just don't shock gobble, even if they've never been called to. Silence doesn't necessarily mean they're not there. Fortunately, if you've done your scouting, you should already know if the birds are present or not and where they'll be going the following morning.

■ There's an old saying that "roosted ain't roasted." Just because you put the birds to bed doesn't mean they'll fly into your lap the next morning. Try to watch them for several days before you hunt to learn their movements.

# PART 2: IMPLEMENTATION

# CHAPTER SIX

# Hunting Roosted Birds

Turkeys were mighty scarce when I started hunting them. In fact, I hunted almost two full seasons before I even came close to shooting one. In that time I learned a lot about how to find them. What I lacked, though, was close-up, personal experience with Ol' Tom. That was about to change one fateful morning as I drove up a steep woods road in the dark.

I pulled into a hemlock grove and checked my watch. Still plenty of time before daylight, so I shut off the engine and cranked the key around so I could listen to the radio. I took a deep gulp of my coffee and was relaxing to the melodic beat of Joan Jett and the Blackhearts singing "I Love Rock N' Roll" when a strange, discordant sound rose in the background.

I killed the radio, opened the window, and heard the unmistakable call of a barred owl, almost on top of me. No sooner had he finished his "who-cooks-for-you-all" cadence when another owl answered from nearby. Then in the distance from the valley below came a different sound.

It was almost surreal. I'd heard turkey gobbles dozens of times on my instructional cassette. But this was the real thing,

an actual, live wild turkey, then another, and another. This was the moment I'd waited two years for, practiced, prepared, dreamed of; now it was finally going to happen. Naturally, I went into full-out panic mode.

Everything I'd learned up to that point, which wasn't much, went right out the window. I scrambled to grab gear from the back of the truck, stuffing calls, gloves, and face mask into the cargo pockets of my military-surplus camo pants. Three steps from the truck I realized I'd forgotten my shells, which only exacerbated my panic. Back to the truck, shells in the gun, then off down the hill. It was like I'd just landed in turkey heaven, and I had to get to those birds before anyone else did.

Halfway down the hill I paused to catch my breath and was nearly knocked down when a tom gobbled from just over a nearby rise. I had barely enough composure to know I should sit, now. I inserted a diaphragm and tried to muster enough saliva to make it work, simultaneously gasping for breath and trying to slow my racing heartbeat. Eventually, I managed to make a sound, and to my absolute amazement,

■ We all dream of the perfect turkey hunt, where a big gobbler pitches out of the roost and struts obligingly into range.

the turkey gobbled back. That was about the last sensible thing I did.

I'd worked so hard to create an opportunity, and now that I had, I didn't have a clue what to do with it. I expected the bird to pop over the rise at any second. When he didn't, doubt filled my head. *I've got to get closer,* I thought. *Maybe just another 20 yards and I'll be able to see over the rise.* I did a quick, low crawl, then backed into the bole of a big oak. "Garobble-obble-obble." He was still there, and there were others nearby.

I called, they gobbled, but they didn't run in as I'd expected. A few more long seconds of anxiety, and I had to move again. The woods went suddenly quiet. I called in desperation, but I knew I'd blown it and was so mad at myself I started back up the hill toward the truck.

That's when I heard a branch snap overhead, followed by the slapping of heavy wings. I looked up to see the sky blackened by an enormous bird taking wing with a large appendage dangling from his breast. *Could it get much worse?* "Boom!" came the blast of a shotgun down in the bottom, offering an immediate answer to my query. I wish I knew then what I know now. That hunt almost certainly would have had a much happier ending, giving me my first turkey and some much-needed confidence. Instead, it would be one more frustrating season before I finally connected.

The purpose of this chapter, and those that follow, is to spare you the same aggravation. While there's no substitute for experience, knowledge and preparation can produce more positive experiences. Having the right tools and knowing how to locate birds are important. But you also need to know what to do with those tools if and when you finally find a potential candidate.

## Off the Roost

We begin this section with the most common scenario: hunting birds off the roost. Whether they roost a bird or birds the evening before or first thing in the morning, most hunters begin their day by hunting roosted birds. The general objective is to sneak in close and early, set up, and call the bird to you. Sound simple? It is, sometimes.

### Step 1: Get In

Immediately, you're asking such questions as "how early should I be there?" and "how close should I get?" The short answer in both cases is "to the greatest extent possible." It's usually advantageous to get in under cover of darkness so you can sneak in unseen. Turkeys have astoundingly good eyesight in daylight but don't seem to do quite so well in darkness or even in the dim gray light of false dawn. In full darkness I've walked within bow range of roosted birds without disturbing them. They still hear well, but there are all sorts of woodland creatures stirring under the roost in the dark, so as long as you don't make too much commotion, the birds don't seem to mind. Obviously, the slower and more quietly you move, the better, which is all the more reason to arrive early. It also helps you beat any potential competitors.

How close you should get is a little more complicated because it really depends on the specific circumstances, and there are so many variables. In general, try to get as close as you can without being heard or seen. If you think there's a chance of either, you're close enough.

You don't want the birds to overfly you. Turkeys leave the roost in many different ways. Some almost drop out of the trees; others may glide 100 yards or more before alighting on the ground. Often they'll have a routine, and if you know it, you can set up accordingly. Otherwise, err on the side of caution, and set up 100 yards or more from the roost.

Be aware of other birds; large flocks roost over large areas. I can't count on two hands the number of times I've slipped in (or attempted to slip in) on a roosted gobbler, only to be busted by hens or jakes roosting 80 or 100 yards away from him.

Other circumstances may also influence your strategy. If you're approaching across a field, for instance, you've got to get settled in extra early and stay a bit farther away. Turkeys may have poor eyesight in dark woods, but they'll pick you out at midnight under a moonlit sky. Early in the season, before leaf-out or in open woods, the birds can see farther. Later, you'll have more cover and can move in closer.

## Step 2: Set Up

Once you're within striking distance, it's time to pick a setup spot. Where you set up can often make or break a hunt. You can increase your odds dramatically if you set up where the birds normally go when they leave the roost; that's when advance scouting comes in handy. You also want to give them a clear path to your location and pick a spot that offers good visibility in front of you. All this applies not only to birds off the roost but to most any setup situation.

Look for a solid background. This too applies to most setup scenarios. For both safety and concealment, try to pick a tree that's at least as wide as your shoulders and as tall as your head (in the case of a dead-fall). You may be there for a while, so it's

■ To have an effective setup, you have to balance sufficient concealment with having good visibility in front of you. I prefer a wide-open view in front. But if you have trouble sitting still, more cover is better.

■ Regardless of the situation, you should always try to set up against a solid background that is wider than your shoulders and taller than your head. This will break up your outline and protect you from the rear.

a good idea to find something fairly comfortable to lean against. Pick a tree that's straight, or even leaning slightly back, but not forward. Also, try to find one with a smooth trunk—no knots or branches to stab you in the back. And check for roots. Somehow they seem to grow the longer you sit.

Now settle in and wait. It's still dark, and it may be a while before the birds come within sight. Adopt a somewhat relaxed posture with your gun in your lap and your legs out straight. If you're far enough

away, you'll still have time to move into the ready position when the time is right.

## Step 3: Calling

Now begins the interactive part of your hunt. All the steps leading up to this are important, but what you do next could be crucial to your success. Unfortunately, there are no hard-and-fast rules. As discussed in chapter four, the amount and type of calling you should do is often reactive and dictated by circumstances, as well as the mood of the bird you're calling.

That being said, hunting off the roost is one of the few situations in which I follow any kind of routine with regard to calling. I begin with a few tree yelps, just to say "good morning" and let the birds know I'm there. Under normal circumstances I won't do much, if any, more calling until almost fly-down time. Exceptions are the rule with turkey hunting, though, and occasionally you get a particularly noisy roost. For whatever reason, the gobblers are firing off, and the hens are making a racket. In this case you have to raise the volume to compete with the real thing.

More often, though, I'll let the birds wake up on their own. When I think fly-down is nearing, I may do a little more tree calling and perhaps a few soft yelps. When it's imminent, or birds are launching from the roost, I might do a fly-down cackle. I believe it's more effective if you can do this before a tom leaves the roost. It tells him, "The hens are lighting out, and they're over this way. If you don't want to get left behind, you'd better come on over."

Once he's on the ground, you should begin your general calling: yelps, clucks, purrs. How much and how often will depend on several factors, including how the bird reacts to your calling, whether he's alone or not, and, if not, the number and sex of birds with him.

Here, as in most calling scenarios, you need to take the bird's "temperature." By that I mean try to gauge his reaction to your calling. If he gets fired up, call more. If not, call less. If he starts your way, call only as much as is necessary to to keep the bird coming in your direction. This is largely opinion based on experience. It may not be what every experienced hunter recommends, but it's worked for me.

There are (at least) two general exceptions to this: If a tom has hens with him, I may call a bit more to outcompete them.

■ **The turkey's eyesight is legendary, and it'll see you long before you see it. That's why you've got to be in position and ready to shoot long before it's in view.**

Also, if he seems to be taking his time or is not very vocal, I may do more soft clucks and purrs, particularly in dense woods, where he may be having trouble locating me. But I don't want to overcall.

## Step 4: Ready, Aim . . .

Whether you can see him or not, before the bird gets close enough to see you, prepare for the shot. This is one of the areas in which hunters often mess up. Remember, a turkey's eyesight is incredibly keen, particularly when it comes to movement. If you're well camouflaged and motionless, they may approach to within feet. Turn your head or lift your gun, and they'll peg you at 100 yards. And they usually don't stick around to see what the movement was.

Long before the bird gets within range or within sight, you need to be in a shooting position. First, face your off-hand shoulder (left if you're a right-hand shooter, and vice versa if you're a southpaw) toward the bird. This allows you more range of motion than facing the bird directly. He may move to the left or right before closing within range, and you want as many options as possible.

Next, prop your gun up on your knee. As he gets closer, you may want to shoulder your gun and even put your cheek to the stock. Don't get caught holding your gun up offhand. Once he's within 75 to 100 yards, you should not move. It may take some time for him to close that final distance, and you want to be as comfortable as possible.

The next-to-last thing to do is take off the safety, and timing is crucial. You don't want the bird to see or hear you do it. Any movement at close range could blow your chance, and yes, I have seen birds react negatively to the "click" of a safety. Before you do this, however, you should be *100 percent certain* of your target. All your efforts are about to pay off, and you're in a very excited, emotional state. In the dawn's early light or the heat of the moment, it's easy to make a mistake. The incident report will call it an accident, but it's not. It's stupidity and carelessness, and it's inexcusable.

Once the bird is in range and in the clear and you're certain of your target and what lies beyond, you have but to pull the trigger. It sounds so simple, yet so many things can go wrong at this point. You wonder how anyone armed with a 12-gauge, 3-inch magnum shotgun could possibly miss a twenty-plus-pound bird at twenty paces, but it happens, more often than we would like.

There are some things you can do to avoid the heartache of a miss. You've patterned your gun, so you know its effective range, but did you practice estimating ranges? Is that bird at 35 yards, or is it more like 55? Do what bowhunters do. Carry a range finder, and measure landmarks ahead of time.

What about the turkey's posture? It's better if you don't shoot a bird in full strut. If using a shotgun, the vital target is the head, which is somewhat protected by the

## CLAIMING YOUR PRIZE

Approach a fallen bird swiftly but safely. First, check that your safety is on. Stand up, and move quickly—don't run—and directly toward the bird. Watch the head; if it's up, be prepared to make a follow-up shot. Don't panic. It is very common for a lethally wounded bird to thrash around wildly. Simply step on its neck until the death throes subside. Don't pick the bird up by its legs until you're sure it's done thrashing.

■ These tactics are intended as general guidelines. Every situation is different. Every encounter is unique. To be consistently successful you'll need to adapt, modify, and overcome.

body when a bird is strutting. You also risk pelletizing the breast meat and blowing off the beard. Wait until the bird has his head up, or make him stick it up with a sharp cluck or putt.

Aim. So many misses are the result of looking over the front sight rather than through it. This lifts your cheek off the stock, causing you to shoot over the bird's head. I speak from experience: *Pull the trigger, you jerk.* Also, squeeze or pull the trigger; don't jerk it. That will only result in a body shot or low miss.

It's a turkey hunter's dream come true. You roost a bird, sneak in before daylight, and set up. At dawn the bird gobbles, and you call. He pitches down and waltzes into range in full strut. A short time later you're at the check station beaming with pride and satisfaction. That's the way we'd all like our hunts to go. But as Scottish poet Robert Burns wrote, "The best laid schemes o' mice an' men gang aft agley." When things don't go quite as planned, you need a Plan B.

# CHAPTER SEVEN

# Tactics and Woodsmanship

This chapter is about tactics and techniques, but I include the term woodsmanship in the title because it is the very fiber that makes up the fabric of successful turkey hunting. Scouting is important, but you need to be able to interpret the sign you find and turn it into something usable. Similarly, tactics and techniques are merely the vocabulary, the raw materials. Woodsmanship is the grammar, applying the raw materials in a logical order and syntax.

## Plan B

I recall one opening day when I blew a bird because I got too close to the roost. Actually, I can recall quite a few, but in

■ As an outdoor writer, I have the singular pleasure of sharing hunting camps with some of the best in the business. We love to compare notes on tips and tactics and what it takes to be a consistently successful turkey hunter. Patience, experience, and familiarity with the terrain are some of the attributes frequently mentioned. In the end, however, the general consensus is that woodsmanship is the single most important attribute of a really good hunter.

this instance I knew where the bird was—or should have been. He evidently moved sometime during the night, because when the sun came up he was perched far from where I saw him fly up and was now almost directly overhead. Furthermore, I had little doubt he had seen and heard me put out the decoys and settle in to my hide because he refused to come down until well after sunup. When he did, he cupped his wings and sailed several hundred yards to the opposite end of the hilltop field before touching down. Then he folded his wings and sneaked into the woods like a kid caught stealing.

Sometimes, for whatever reason, you don't kill a bird right out of the roost. I could write an entire book of examples from personal experience. Maybe they weren't responding to the calls, someone interfered with you, or you got too tight to the roost. Regardless, your hunt is far from over, provided of course you have a Plan B. I didn't. At least, I didn't have a backup location on hand for just such an instance. That meant I had to improvise.

■ Just because they don't gobble doesn't mean they're not there. Birds will often come in silently, so you should always be alert when calling.

There was not a gobble to be heard. Even if there had been, I probably wouldn't have heard it over the thirty-knot winds. But I knew the place held birds and the woodlot below the field would be more sheltered. So off I went, into the woods and down the first slope. Stopping at the first bench, I listened intently for a gobble. No luck. Many hunters would have given up at that point and moved on to greener pastures. But I had an idea.

## Calling Blind

I didn't get involved in the sport until several decades after the resurgence of modern spring turkey hunting; when I did, I studied both contemporary and traditional tactics. This situation called for one of the latter that is often referred to as "yelp three times on a box call, then wait half an hour" or, simply, "blind calling."

Nobody really knows why, but there are some days when the birds just won't gobble, and you'd swear there isn't a turkey within 10 miles. We know better. Just because they don't gobble doesn't mean they're not there. You should already know this from scouting; if you've seen birds in the area recently or noticed fresh sign, there's a good chance there are turkeys within hearing distance. Park your carcass and start calling.

But don't be too hasty to sit. If you're going to invest the time to sit for several hours, you should invest it wisely. This is where woodsmanship comes in. Look for places that offer good visibility for you and ease of travel for turkeys. Small benches and saddles in hilly terrain are ideal. Turkeys are more visible in open habitat, but they spend far more time under the cover of trees, if the terrain allows it. Look for narrow wooded funnels that connect larger blocks, just as you would for deer. A good woodsman can read the terrain and recognize and avoid obstacles such as creeks, steep slopes, and dense thickets, which may stop an incoming bird short of your position. And, of course, scout the sign. Fresh scratching in a feeding area suggests the birds will be along again at some point.

One of my favorite blind-calling spots is a dust bowl. You'll recall from chapter five that, after an active morning of feeding, turkeys sometimes take a dust bath—presumably to rid themselves of parasites. They find a hollowed-out depression in dry soil and roll in it, using their wings to throw dirt over themselves. Turkeys often use the same bowls on a regular basis, which makes them great places to set up when the birds aren't cooperating.

You should also be particular about exactly where you plop down. As mentioned in the previous chapter, it can sometimes tip the odds in your favor. In time you'll develop an instinct for recognizing a good setup location. Meanwhile, follow a few general rules. Give the birds and yourself an opening; turkeys are woodland creatures, but they avoid areas with a dense understory, where predators may

■ Take cues from other woodland creatures. If a squirrel suddenly starts barking at some unseen movement in the brush, get ready. It could be Ol' Tom.

lurk. You, meanwhile, want a good view and a clear shot.

However, you have to balance that with being concealed. Some hunters prefer to have more cover immediately in front of them. They may use natural cover or find a few branches to form a quick, makeshift ground blind. This is a better option for younger hunters or others who have difficulty sitting still. I prefer not to have anything in front of me that might limit my visibility, inhibit me from moving my gun, or otherwise interfere with a shot—but I can sit rock still for long periods of time.

Speaking of sitting still, you should always be still and alert, but this is especially true when blind calling. Obviously, you're looking and listening for turkeys, but other creatures can also offer cues worth noting. Nothing passes in the woods unnoticed. Crows flying overhead can't seem to resist swooping down low over turkeys and alerting all within earshot to their presence. If a nearby squirrel or songbird suddenly starts barking out alarm calls, get ready. They could be announcing the imminent arrival of a longbeard.

## Keys to Effective Communication

When dealing with turkeys, as with people, success often lies with effective communication. That involves saying the right thing at the right time, which we discussed to some extent in chapter four. As previously mentioned, much of calling is reactive, responding appropriately to a bird that answers you. And often each situation calls for a specific response. Still, there are some guidelines you can follow.

Regardless of the circumstances, it's a good idea to begin by calling softly, in case there are birds close by. If you get no response, call a little louder. If that gets no reply, you still have several options. One is to adopt the old-school strategy and simply wait a while before calling again.

In the aforementioned situation I opted for another. After settling in for what I expected to be a long wait and laying out all my calls, I started with a box. No reply. Next, I picked up a slate and hammered on it. Still no sound. Then I switched mouth calls and tried a raspier tone. I hadn't even finished my staccato cutting when a loud gobble boomed back just downslope. Two more calling bouts, and ten minutes later the bird lay at my feet.

Option one might have worked had I been patient enough. Though he didn't gobble, there's a good possibility that bird might still have come to the call. Birds often come in silently on those quiet days, which is why you always have to be alert when calling. Option two worked in this case, though another day it might not have. Then again, I could have explored a third option: move to another location. Simply moving to a new location and setting up to call blind is still old school. How much and how often you move should be on a gradual scale, but at some point it represents a paradigm shift to a more aggressive hunting style known as running and gunning, which we'll cover in the next chapter.

The same logic that applies to volume also applies to intensity. Begin by calling modestly. Make your presence known without intimidating your quarry. See how the bird responds; take his temperature. Then, as discussed in chapter four, respond accordingly. If he wants to start a shouting match, pour it on. If he just wants to stay in contact, keep talking.

Again, determining the right amount of calling can be a crap shoot. Some of that knowledge comes with experience and confidence. It also helps if you try to keep it real.

I call a lot, but most of my calling is soft and subtle. Rather than cranking on a box call to imitate an excited hen—something you rarely hear—I try to sound like a real turkey or a group of turkeys contentedly feeding along. Sometimes it's hard to stick to soft purrs, clucks, and scratching in the leaves when a tom double and triple gobbles. But if he's headed your way, it may be the best option. It also helps keep him interested without overcalling. Still, there are times when you just can't help yourself, and you get one of those suicidal, masochistic turkeys that love to be shouted at. It can make for a very exciting and often brief hunt.

## Closing the Distance

If deciding how much to call is the turkey hunter's toughest decision, deciding how close to get is the second toughest. On the conservative side, if the bird can hear you, it's possible to call him in. On the aggressive side the closer you get, the better your odds of calling him in. Your best odds lie in getting as close as you can, without being seen or heard (turkeys will shy away from the sound of you crashing through the underbrush).

Here again, there are no hard-and-fast rules, but circumstances often dictate what to do. Early in the season, before leaf-out or in more open habitat, you can see and hear a long way, and so can the turkeys. They might be a bit more eager to come to the call as well. In this situation you may need to hang back a little. Later in the season or in thicker cover, vegetation inhibits both sight and sound. If you can hear a bird clearly now, you might want to think about sitting where you are.

It also helps if you can get a few gobbles out of the bird before committing. That way you can track him. If he's headed your way, you may want to sit down and call from where you are, even if he's still a ways off. If he seems hung up, you may be able to get closer. And if he's moving off,

you could try to get out in front. Remember, it's always easier to call a bird to you if you're where he wants to go anyway.

## Decoys

Decoys are another way to coax a bird your way. An entire chapter could be written on their use; in fact, I had originally planned to do just that. I finally decided it wouldn't be fair to other sections of the book that were equally deserving of just as much space, so what follows is a lengthy segment on what to use, how and when to use them, and even whether to use them at all.

We'll start with the last question first. They're by no means a necessity. Folks have been killing turkeys in Alabama for decades, and decoys were only recently legalized there. Decoys add weight and bulk to your vest, and there's no question that on rare occasions they will intimidate turkeys. That being said, I've had so much success using decoys that I rarely hunt without them.

Which type I use often depends on how I hunt. If I'm running and gunning, I prefer lighter, more compact versions, such as two-dimensional silhouettes. In a more sedentary setup, I'll often opt for the added realism of three-dimensional ones, usually the collapsible-foam or rubber models. However, there's no doubt in my mind that "stuffers"—taxidermy mounts of real birds—are far more effective than any other type.

■ They're pricey, bulky, and delicate, but authentic "stuffer" decoys clearly outshine all other types when it comes to fooling the real thing.

What to use? It's spring mating season, and the object is to lure a tom by exploiting his lust, jealousy, or sometimes both. A single hen decoy will work, but often a pair work better. They add a visual component to your calling, and it's what that tom is looking for. Throw in a jake, and you add an element of competition. In fact, a jake and two hens has almost become the industry standard in turkey decoys.

Circumstances sometimes dictate your layout. For instance, field setups beg for some kind of decoy. Turkeys can see a long way across open ground, and field birds can be particularly stubborn if they don't have a visual cue. The standard one- or three-bird set will work, though conditions may call for more creativity. When hunting in a windrow between two fields, for example, I'll often bring more decoys so I can set some in each field. You can do the same when hunting the break from open woods to field edge. Place some in the woods and some in the field, especially if the field is not visible from the woods because of fences, stone walls, or thicker vegetation that often grows along field edges.

Field birds are often considered tough to hunt. They become even harder when they're with hens, which we'll discuss in more detail later in the book. There are a couple of things you can do with decoys that may turn the tide. One is to adopt the goose hunter's philosophy that more is better. When hunting henned-up field toms, I may occasionally set out as many as six or eight decoys. This "confidence flock" helps put edgy birds at ease. Among them will be my other ace card, a strutting tom or jake.

Full-strut decoys have been around for years but have really caught on only recently. I'm not sure why it took so long, because they can be downright deadly. You typically get one of two reactions from a tom: They either shy away or throw caution to the wind and head straight to it, sometimes on a dead run. You can always play it safe and use a half-strut or relaxed male decoy. Speaking of safety, it should always be your number-one priority when using any type of tom or jake decoy. While it should never happen, it is possible someone could mistake your decoy for the real thing.

■ Full-strut tom decoys are all the rage now and with good reason. Toms will often approach them with reckless abandon.

## Poses and Positions

How you place your decoys can also make a great deal of difference. When using the standard three-decoy rig, for instance, place the jake closest to you, and leave a space and your best shooting lane between it and the hens. An approaching tom will almost always go to the jake decoy first, trying to separate it from the hens. If you know from which direction a bird is likely to approach—on a field edge, for example—place the decoys off to one side or the other, to your left if you're right-handed and vice versa. This will divert an approaching bird's attention away from your position.

I also face my decoys in the direction I want the turkey to go. It may be pure hooey, but I believe it works. Turkeys are gregarious by nature and have a tendency to follow other turkeys for no other reason than to be with them. If my decoys are facing an approaching tom, he may be less inclined to come all the way in than if he perceives the flock to be moving away.

Seeing a potential rival with hens appeals to the jealous nature of a tom. But seeing a jake or another tom breeding a hen

■ When both are present, a tom will almost always approach a jake or tom decoy before that of a hen.

absolutely drives him wild. Several decoy manufacturers now make decoys that can be positioned in the breeding posture, with the jake on top of the hen. If you don't own them, you can position your own decoys in the same way. A hen squats to be bred, so stake a hen at ground level. Then stake a jake on top, and slightly to the rear. You'll be amazed how effective this posture is. Sometimes even a single hen placed in the breeding position will work.

## Location

Oftentimes where you set up is just as important as how you set up. As mentioned earlier, the key to hunting field birds is visibility—making your decoys as visible as possible. If there's any terrain, try to set up on a high spot, so your decoys can be seen from any direction and from a long way off. Another good field setup is at the point where a finger or corner of woods juts into the field. This affords your decoys greater visibility and you more field of fire.

I use somewhat the opposite theory when setting up in the woods. I don't want the bird to see my decoys until he's close. In thicker woods turkeys can't see well anyway and are coming more to the call than any visual stimulus. I believe they're more inclined to keep coming if they have

to search harder for the decoy. When they finally find it, the decoy is already within their confidence area, so closing the distance is a mere formality, and the decoy diverts their attention away from you.

## Motion

Anything that creates a more realistic situation puts birds more at ease, and that includes adding movement to your decoys. Even the simplest decoys are designed to spin or rock on their stakes. To keep them from spinning too much on windy days, you can poke a few sticks in the ground on either side. Some come with movable heads that bob in the wind or that you attach to monofilament fishing line. Tugging on the line makes the decoy's head tip, simulating feeding. More elaborate examples are suspended on retractable wires, and some can even be moved by remote control.

This and the previous chapter should have given you a broad overview of the basics—at least enough to get you started with confidence. So much of turkey hunting is reactive and dependent on current conditions, climate, habitat, and your mood and that of the birds you pursue. The next few chapters will provide some advice on more specific circumstances so that ultimately you'll be ready for just about anything that comes your way.

# CHAPTER EIGHT

# Running and Gunning

I freely admit that I will never be a great turkey hunter. I lack the necessary patience. Some of that may be because I spend so much time in the fall sitting in trees waiting for the deer that never comes. It's also quite possibly, at least in part, the result of the much-faster-paced lifestyle we all lead these days. Regardless of the reasons, when nothing's happening I feel the need to get up and make something happen. And I'm not alone. This more contemporary hunting style is part of a larger category of tactics often referred to as running and gunning. I really don't know whether it has better odds. I just prefer to be moving.

## Trolling

As mentioned in the chapter on woodsmanship, tactics vary on a continuum as you gradually transition from sitting and calling to getting up and moving. At the most basic level is a technique sometimes referred to as trolling. It consists basically of moving along slowly and trying to make a bird gobble. It's a lot like still-hunting for deer. You move slowly and quietly enough

so you might hear or see a distant bird before giving yourself away. How often you stop and call is a matter of personal preference, but I usually go about 100 yards between bouts. Here again, I'll start calling softly, then increase the volume if I get no response.

The object here, as with roosting, is to make a bird gobble and thus give away his presence and location. It is often advantageous if you can do so by using a nonturkey call, such as for an owl or a woodpecker; the turkey gives away his position without really attracting his attention to yours. This allows you to move into a better position, if needed, before you try calling him closer. That being said, you'll raise far more shock gobbles by using a turkey call. Sometimes you just gotta weigh the odds.

Again, type and volume will vary with conditions, but I typically use the loudest call in my vest—a box or a slate. I'll do two or three bouts, listening in between. If I get no response, I move another 100 yards or so and try it again.

Before I call, I always take a quick look around. I want to be ready in case I do get a response, so I look for favorable conditions:

a good back rest with enough cover for me but open enough in front that I can see any approaching birds. I also do a lot of listening. Sometimes you can hear distant yelps or clucks or birds scratching in the leaves. When a bird does respond, you go into action, setting up and calling as described in previous chapters.

## Watch Your Back

How far and in which direction you should travel can vary with circumstances and personal preference. At some point you'll have to turn around and return to your point of origin.

You can go a different route in hopes of finding fresh ground and new birds, or you can retrace your steps. Given the choice, I'll usually take the latter. If you're on good ground, there are birds present, and they likely heard your calling. Furthermore, turkeys have an uncanny ability to pinpoint a calling location. While they may not come right away, there's a good chance they will eventually investigate. Far too often for it to be mere coincidence, I've bumped into birds on my return trip that were at or near places I'd previously called from.

## End Around

From the time they hit the ground in the morning until they fly up to roost at night, turkeys are on the move. If you happen

■ When to sit tight and when it's time to make a move can be one of the toughest decisions a turkey hunter must make. That knowledge will only come with experience.

to be ahead of them, your odds of calling them to the gun are much better. Quite often, though, you'll encounter a gobbling bird that's moving away from you. Because it's rare that a bird will turn around and retrace its steps, returning to a place it just left, if you want to do battle, your only choice is an end around.

The first obvious step is to determine his direction of travel. Next, circle out wide enough so as not to spook him or any birds in his company. This all sounds easy, but it isn't. Turkeys can travel surprisingly

■ When trying to shock a bird into gobbling, it's often a good idea to use a nonturkey call, such as that of a crow, woodpecker, or coyote.

fast when they're feeding and even faster when they're heading to a feeding area. Furthermore, to avoid the turkey's legendary eyesight, you have to make a wide loop out and around, which means you'll have to cover a lot more ground than he does. You've got to be in shape, particularly if you're in hilly terrain.

Here's another problem: You need to keep tabs on the bird's location, which you can do if he keeps gobbling. If he stops, however, you've got to make him gobble. Again, this is best done with shock calls of crows, woodpeckers, or coyotes. Save the turkey calls for when you're in position.

Your next move is critical, and it's where most hunters mess up. If you think you've gone far enough to get in front of the bird, go a little farther. You're excited, the adrenaline is pumping, and most hunters have a tendency to cut in too soon. Give yourself plenty of margin for error. And shift gears. Stop; calm yourself. Stand another ten to fifteen seconds, and listen for another gobble. If the bird is still moving ahead or seems to veer away from your calling, loop out in front again, set up quickly, and wait silently. If, on the other hand, the bird stops and begins gobbling from a fixed position, it's time to set up and start calling. If he hangs up—continues to call but won't come closer—you may have to apply one of the advanced tactics covered in the chapter on tough toms (see chapter ten).

■ When hunting big, open country, ATVs are a great way to get out ahead of moving birds.

## I Can See for Miles

If you're hunting in open country, you can adapt these strategies by borrowing a page from the mule deer hunter's handbook and try a little spot and stalk. You begin by glassing from hills or bluffs and listening for gobbles. Just as with the end-around method, your objective is to try to determine where the bird is going and get there ahead of him. There won't be much vegetation to use for cover, so you'll have to rely mainly on topography. Small hills can sometimes afford enough cover. These areas are also frequently laced with narrow ravines, which also offer a topographical advantage and often have some degree of vegetative cover. Here, binoculars take on added importance. It's also helpful to pick out some feature to use as a landmark as you proceed. Caution is also advised, as this is rattlesnake country.

Even in open forest you have to be careful about how you approach. A bird can spot you from a long way off moving down the side of an open hardwood ridge. If he's on top, which he most likely will be, you've got to get below him and use the topography as cover. Once

■ Compact binoculars are handy anywhere but become especially important when running and gunning in open country.

you're in the bottoms, you can move on a more direct path toward the bird. Try to approach along as steep a route as possible; it will provide more concealment from above, and a bird is less likely to come toward you.

While it's not always true, a general rule of thumb is that it's easier to call a bird uphill. Thus, you should try to get above the bird if at all possible. Of course, if the bird is moving down, you need to do likewise, as you won't be able to turn him back up.

## Take Me to the River

If the area you hunt has rivers or large streams and you're not using them, you're overlooking a great run-and-gun opportunity. Most hunters access their hunting areas by land. Going by boat, however, offers several advantages. First, waterways provide easy access to areas that may otherwise be difficult, if not impossible, to get to on foot. Second, you can come in from a direction different from the way most hunters approach, potentially offering an element of surprise. Third, you can cover more ground with less effort and move fast if you need to.

There are several ways to go about it, but a typical scenario begins by motoring up- or downriver, away from the crowds, well before daylight. Then just sit and listen. In areas where high banks and running water sometimes make it difficult to hear, climb up on the bank and listen. When you hear a bird, motor (or paddle) up as close as you can without spooking it, set up, and begin calling. If something goes wrong with that bird, jump in the boat and go find another one. You won't be able to hear gobbling over the din of the motor, so you should cut the engine every quarter mile or so and listen. You can even do some crow or turkey calling to try to elicit a shock gobble.

This boating method also can be done by canoe. The best way is to have two vehicles: Park one at the downstream end of your hunt, then drive up to the launch and float downstream. While it's slower and requires a bit more effort, you'll be virtually silent and can call and listen as you go. Here too you need to be cautious of snakes in some areas, particularly water moccasins, which like to loaf on limbs overhanging the river. This technique works best early in the day, while the birds are still in the bottoms, before they move out into the fields.

## Conclusion

Some purists may look down upon some of the techniques discussed in this chapter. They're certainly entitled to their viewpoint and opinion. But I for one am not out in the woods to commune with nature. I'm there to kill a turkey and will use whatever legal and ethical means are available to me. Besides, it takes just as much skill in woodsmanship to maneuver within range of a gobbler as it does to call one into range. And though you may blow some opportunities by being aggressive, you will also create more for yourself. In time you'll learn when to be aggressive and when to mellow out.

# CHAPTER NINE

# Teaming Up

In my early years I did the overwhelming majority of my turkey hunting alone. Oh, I'd often be with other hunters, but when it came time to hit the woods, we went our separate ways until the day's hunt was concluded. I preferred it that way, mostly because I didn't know any differently. When I started guiding, I learned that successfully calling in a bird was equally rewarding, regardless of who ultimately pulled the trigger. And I had the added thrill of seeing many folks kill their first turkey. This in turn got me pairing up with other hunters—friends and fellow outdoor writers—on a more regular basis. Looking back now, I realize how much I

■ Hunting with a partner can not only be advantageous, but also a lot more fun.

■ Having one hunter as the designated caller allows the other to concentrate on being ready to shoot without having to move.

missed by hunting solo so many years. I've also learned that it is far more than a matter of companionship or preference. Pairing up can actually increase your chances of being successful, and this chapter will explain how.

## Hands Up

I can recall one morning hunting the edge of a corn-stubble field where I'd observed several birds regularly feeding on waste grain. It was shortly after daylight when my calling elicited a loud gobble from the adjacent woodlot. The bird thundered back each time I struck my slate, but his progress in my direction was infinitesimally slow. Then he went silent for several minutes. I should have known better, but because he had been responding so well, I continued to call. Suddenly, without warning, the bird stepped out of the thicket and into the open field a mere 30 yards away. My eyes shifted from the bird to my hands, both of which were ineffectually occupied with a slate and peg. As if to mock me, the bird moved to within 25 yards before disappearing back into the woods.

Unless calling exclusively with a diaphragm, at some point the solo hunter will have to make a decision as to when is the right time to lay down your call and pick up your gun. This can be a pretty dicey situation. Do it too soon, and the bird may lose interest, while your arms tire and your muscles cramp. Wait too long, and you'll end up like I did, or you'll get caught moving to raise your gun.

Hunting in tandem eliminates this problem. When guiding, I typically do all the calling for my hunters. As soon as I sense a bird is moving in, I'll instruct them to get their gun up on a knee, point it in the bird's direction, and be ready. Meanwhile, I can continue to use both hands on slates, box calls, or whatever's necessary to coax the bird into range, sometimes using multiple calls at once. When the bird appears, the hunter is ready to shoot. Because many of my clients are first-time hunters or novices, I usually sit close by. More experienced tandem hunters using this technique may want to position the shooter a short distance in front of the caller. More on that later.

## Left-Handed Turkeys

Gobblers, especially the older, warier variety, are notorious for circling rather than coming directly to a call. They also seem to have an uncanny knack for knowing whether the shooter is right- or left-handed. I'm a right-handed shooter, and it would take both hands to count the number of times I've had birds come in on my right side, where even lightning-quick calisthenics couldn't get me into shooting position before the bird vanished. For the solo hunter the only recourse is to wait it out and hope the turkey circles around, still in range.

Teaming up allows you to double your field of fire, covering a bird's approach from several different directions. Under the right conditions, and with right- and left-handed shooters, you can even cover 360 degrees, ensuring a shot no matter what direction a bird approaches from.

It also allows you a greater field of vision without movement, which is critical when the birds get in close. Shoulder to shoulder, two hunters can whisper status and instructions back and forth, eliminating the temptation to peer over your shoulder and possibly spook a bird.

One morning I was calling to a particularly stubborn trio of birds, trying to pull them within range of a client. They were too close to allow a move on our part, but they refused to close the distance. Our attention was riveted on the trio when I heard the soft footfalls of a turkey sneaking in behind us, as they so often do.

By the time I heard it, it was too late. "Don't move," I whispered. My muscles strained to hold still, and I fought off the urge to slap a mosquito chewing away at my ear. Out of the corner of my eye, I could see my companion's chest heaving from excitement as he fought to control his breath. The bird came closer and closer, finally stopping feet from us. Then came the unmistakable alarm putt—he had nailed us. Figuring the jig was up anyway, I turned in time to see the red-headed long-beard vanish into the underbrush. Had another shooter been facing that way, the bird would have made an easy target.

## Doubling Up

Having two guns can also sometimes afford both hunters an opportunity to tag out in quick order, provided they're prepared. Several years ago I experienced a perfect example—of what not to do. I was tag-team hunting with a friend. We'd roosted a bird the night before and agreed ahead that he would be the caller and I the shooter. The gobbler serenaded us from the roost just before dawn, and we moved into position. I put out a pair of decoys and sat down against the bole of a big tree. My partner moved about 15 yards back, set his gun on his lap, and pulled out his calls.

The setup seemed perfect. My partner began some soft calling, and before long I saw the red, white, and blue of the gobbler's head approaching from just over the next rise. Then things started getting confusing. More heads and bodies appeared. Gun up, I focused on the first tom, ignoring the others. When he crossed that magic line, I squeezed off a shot, and he crumpled. One of the other birds, confused by the commotion, began putting and nervously walking closer. He passed by me at 20 yards, then continued on toward my friend, quartering by to his left at a mere 15 yards. I awaited the shot that never came. Later, he related that he was so surprised at the bird's approach he froze and couldn't lift his gun to shoot.

This was hardly an isolated episode. In spring, after the winter flocks break up and breeding season begins, toms begin to segregate themselves as they sort out the pecking order. At the top of the totem is the boss tom, who does most of the breeding. Just below him are younger males who travel in small sibling groups. Thus, you'll often see several toms of the same age traveling together. Like satellite bulls in an elk herd, these frustrated subordinates circle the fringes of the boss's harem looking for an opportunity to sneak in a quickie, so they are much more susceptible to calling.

When your calling elicits multiple gobbling, you may want to redirect your field of fire to a smaller area. Set up as close to one another as possible, at least within conversational distance. In this way you can exchange instructions as to who shoots which bird and when to shoot. Countless times I've had other toms linger after one of their comrades had fallen, and more than once I literally had to chase birds away from a fallen tom after the shot and wished I had another hunter, or another tag, with me.

## Hang-Ups

Birds hanging up just beyond gun range is probably the number-one nemesis of turkey hunters. Sometimes they'll respond to your every cluck and yelp, but then for some reason they hit a wall, beyond which they will not tread. Some hunters speculate the tom is looking for the source of the calling and, seeing no hen, refuses to advance. Others conjecture it is the nature of the bird for the hen to come to the tom rather than vice versa. The latter is probably closer to reality. In nature it is usually the hen who comes to the tom, and it is instinct rather than reason that causes the gobblers to hold tight. Either way, it can be a frustrating situation.

This is where a pair of hunters can really be effective. The shooter remains in position while the caller moves directly away from the tom. The theory is that thinking he's hearing the hen moving away the gobbler will advance; the same tactic works when rattling whitetails. Because his attention is riveted on the caller, the tom will sometimes run right over the shooter.

This tactic is most effective if you can keep the shooter directly between the caller and the gobbler. This may require the caller to move left or right as the bird moves right or left. It also helps if both hunter and caller are experienced, as safety must be stressed. Once you move out of sight of the shooter, your calling is all he has to mark your location. If there is no shot, you should have some sort of signal, such as a whistle, that it is safe for you to return.

## Stakeouts

Preseason scouting and patterning birds is one way to significantly increase your chances of bringing home a butterball. But like mature bucks, some old toms are downright unpatternable. One morning they'll leave the roost and go one way, the next day they'll capriciously go another. By splitting up your two-man team, you can cover two possible travel routes, doubling the odds of someone being in the right place.

Again, when doing this it is very important to hunt with someone you are familiar and comfortable with and to have a plan and stick with it, no matter what. You must constantly be certain of one another's location to avoid an accident. Once separated, do not move, unless it's part of the plan. Intermittent calling will also reassure your partner of your location. However, calling can sometimes have the opposite of the desired effect, particularly in areas of heavy hunting pressure. Under these circumstances it is sometimes the silent hunter who gets the shot as the bird sneaks away from the caller.

Another variation of the stakeout I discovered somewhat by accident. We were hunting a transmission-line right-of-way, a favorite travel route for turkeys, and it was one of those slow days. After an hour of calling from one location, we packed up the decoys and moved down the line a quarter mile or so. The terrain was hilly, so I could see across a broad valley back to our previous location on a facing hill.

We had been calling for maybe twenty minutes when I noticed a black shape across the valley. My binoculars revealed a discouraging sight: A big tom had come out onto the right-of-way and was slowly ambling past the location of our previous calling bout.

Though he took us by surprise, this behavior is not all that unusual. In late morning, after peak feeding activity ends, the hens go to brood their clutches, but toms are still looking for love. They may not be the most intelligent creatures in the world, but they have fairly good memories and will often return to where they heard calling earlier in the day.

I usually reserve this tactic for those really slow days, when nothing will raise a gobble: It takes a great deal of patience for one of your pair to stay behind—after

■ Turkeys don't usually travel alone, so why should we? My kids both tagged out on Maine's youth day hunt when a flock of three gobblers came in.

you've given up all hope on a location—while the other moves on to a new spot. Even worse for the guy left behind, this tactic seems to work best if he does not call.

## Different Strokes

Veteran turkey hunters know sometimes it takes just the right call to fire up a reluctant old gobbler. When acting as a guide, I carry a variety of different calls: slates, box calls, diaphragms, just in case. Having two hunters doubles the number of potential calls available should you be forced to go through your entire arsenal searching for the "right" call. Having a bushel of calls also offers another advantage.

## Flocking

Sometimes a little understanding of turkey biology can go a long way toward hunting success. Turkeys are gregarious, enjoying the company of others of their kind. They are also polygamous, which means one male will breed several hens from his harem. It necessarily follows then that the sound of multiple hens will be more likely to attract a reluctant tom than that of a single hen. According to "the American way," more is better. Logically then, if a solo hunter using multiple calls works well, two hunters doing the same should work better. I've partnered up using this technique successfully several times.

We usually hold this tactic back for those times when conventional methods don't work, after we've thrown every call in our vest at a wary old tom and he still won't come. I've used two variations. The first involves imitating a flock of feeding hens. Each of us will use multiple calls while simultaneously scratching the leaves. Often that's enough to push a hesitant old tom over the edge. When it's not, we switch to fighting purrs.

This call, designed to imitate sparring rival males, can be used by a solo hunter but is even more realistic and effective when used by two hunters. It's especially effective if you're not necessarily after the boss tom. Just like kids on a playground, no adolescent turkey can resist a fight, and jakes are especially vulnerable to the fighting-purrs call. Someone's getting his butt kicked, and this might be a chance for them to move up in the pecking order. I've even purred jakes into range after getting caught standing in the open.

## Companionship

In addition to increasing the number and type of tactics available, hunting with a partner offers one more very important thing—companionship. Many hunters cite camaraderie as one of the major reasons they hunt. Having someone else there to swap ideas and share the outdoor experience with makes it that much more enjoyable. It's also a great way to introduce new or young hunters to the sport. Whether you're looking to boost your odds of putting a turkey dinner in the oven or you merely want someone to share the experience with, try doubling up.

■ Hunting with companions gives you a chance to bounce ideas off one another when you're uncertain what your next move should be.

# CHAPTER TEN

# Tough Toms

Beginner's luck can sometimes be a curse, particularly for a turkey hunter. I was fortunate enough never to suffer that malady; my first birds were agonizingly difficult. But I've seen enough beginners to recognize the symptoms. Their first time out they find one of those dumb birds, those naive two-year-olds that will run to anything that sounds remotely like a hen turkey. The bird blunders in on a kamikaze run, and our nimrod, almost in self-defense, pulls the trigger. Fooled into thinking they've outwitted the king of game birds, they confidently boast how easy turkey hunting is. They may even pull off this feat more than once. But reality will soon come as a cold, hard slap in the face.

Eventually they're going to come up against a bird that represents a challenge, and unless they've earned their scars and stripes, they won't be prepared for it. They come in many guises, those tough toms, each with its own set of problems. What follows are some of the more common scenarios involving more challenging birds.

## Foul-Weather Fowl

Patience is one of the most important qualities of a successful turkey hunter, and it takes on extra importance in bad weather. In economic terms a turkey's survival is based on a cost-benefit ratio. He needs food (benefits) to attain his priority, which is survival. There is a cost associated with acquiring that food; namely, burning calories and exposing himself to danger. Those costs go up significantly during poor weather. On rainy days everything's colder, darker, and wetter. On windy days the woods are full of noise and movement that can overload the turkey's acute danger-detection senses. The combination of moisture and wind also draws valuable energy, in the form of body heat, away from him. To compensate (reduce costs), the bird spends more time on the roost early in the day, preening wet feathers and waiting until it's light enough to see predators. He may even forgo more trivial matters such as mating if the weather's particularly bad. During heavy rain the bird may not move at all. Those are the days for the hunter to stay home. During a light rain, however, the turkey can usually gain enough calories to compensate. Unless it's extremely cold, he's much more likely to move on windy days. Either way he'll get a late start.

That's why you need to be patient. Don't expect the birds to fly down at first light, though they might. Set up as you normally would, but be prepared to wait longer, much longer, if they don't show up right away. This is not a day to move around and call. It's a day to camp out.

Camping calls for a tent, and so does hunting in the rain. This is the perfect scenario for a portable, pop-up blind. Bring along a folding chair and enough food and clothing to make yourself comfortable, and plan on spending the day. It may take longer than usual, but if you've chosen your location well, the birds will be along eventually.

■ I used to hate hunting turkeys in the rain. Then I discovered pop-up blinds and realized that if I set up on the edge of a field and waited patiently, I could hunt in relative comfort and with little competition.

When picking a spot, think "open." During bad weather, turkeys tend to prefer open areas, where predator detection is easier. Forget about the traditional strutting areas in the woods. Concentrate on open areas, such as prairies, meadows, agricultural fields, or recent cutovers.

As their other main priority is eating, they'll also be in the areas of greatest food concentration. Places like a corn-stubble field offer the perfect combination of open area and high-calorie food. If no such areas exist where you hunt, look for mature hardwood stands, especially nut-bearing trees such as oak and beech, with an open understory.

Rainy days are also a good time to catch up on some much-needed rest. The birds will be late in moving, and what few hunters go out don't usually stay out long. You can sleep in, then go out and have the best spots to yourself. Furthermore, if the first wave of hunters did any calling, toms may already have your location "earmarked" for investigation.

Windy days offer a somewhat different set of circumstances. Turkeys are just as likely to stick to the open areas as on nonwindy days, but they're more likely to vocalize. The problem is you can't hear them and they can't hear you. Rather than sitting tight, you may be better off moving. Covering more ground will increase your chances of locating a gobbling bird, and with all the movement in the woods, you may not get caught should you stumble upon a gobbler accidentally. Of course

safety is especially important, and you should wear at least one object of orange clothing when moving.

You can also call birds in on windy days, but you'll need the right calls. Diaphragms and softer calls just don't have what it takes to cut through the roar of the wind. For starters I use larger "boat paddle"–type box calls or synthetic slates made of Plexiglass or aluminum—the louder the better. If you get a bird to start coming, you can always switch to a softer call when he gets closer.

As I mentioned, open areas are the best places to look. Skirt the edges of fields, staying inside the tree line, and glass with high-powered binoculars. Again, the wind will help cover your movement. If there are no open areas where you hunt, head for the high ground. Walking ridgetops will allow you to hear farther, and you can cover two valleys simultaneously. Another place to concentrate your efforts is on the leeward side of hills and ridges. Birds will often move to such areas to get out of the wind.

Another reason to hunt on stormy days is that eventually the bad weather will pass. If you happen to be afield when it does, look out. Turkeys subdued by inclement weather will be anxious to get back to their routine, and feeding and breeding will sometimes reach a frenzied level shortly after a fast-moving front has passed.

## Henned-Up Birds

Henned-up birds are the greatest nemesis of the spring turkey hunter. (There's only

**A harem of hens pulled this bird off the roost and away from my insistent calling. I held tight, and two hours later he came back looking for me.**

one type of turkey more challenging, which we'll talk about in chapter eleven.) The entire premise of spring turkey hunting is to lure a lovesick tom into range by imitating that which he most wants: a hen. Once he's got the real thing, calling becomes more of a challenge. And the more hens he gathers into his harem, the harder he is to call. Fortunately, there are remedies.

Turkeys don't have emotions. Eons of evolution have programmed their minuscule bird brains to react to stimuli. However, in order to explain some of their

■ Hunter's Specialties pro-staffer Rick White and I encountered this henned-up Oklahoma gobbler at first light. He refused to come to the call, and it took us almost five hours to finally maneuver into position for a shot.

behavior to humans, we sometimes need to cheat a little and apply human terms, such as lust and jealousy. If turkeys did have emotions, those would be a tom's two strongest in spring. His goal is to mate and in doing so to drive off any rivals.

The same logic applies to hens. If you'll excuse further anthropomorphism, hens also have a jealous bone. Piss them off, and they're likely to do one of two things. They'll either lead their tom in the opposite direction, or they'll come over to kick your butt and in the process bring the tom with them. That's why you may be more effective calling his hens.

You can usually tell early on if it's gonna work. You call, and a hen answers. That's a good sign. You call some more, and she answers again, this time more emphatically. That's a better sign. As long as she keeps answering, you should keep calling; and don't be afraid to ramp it up if she sounds increasingly more agitated. That's exactly what you want. Bear in mind, however, that the odds are equally good she will take her man and the rest of the flock, turn directly away, and head off for parts unknown.

Another technique for henned-up toms is what I call a rain check. Early in the morning he's got his harem, and he could care less about some stray bird in the bush. As the day winds on, hens begin to drop out of the flock to tend their nests. By mid- to late morning the hens are gone, and the toms redouble their efforts at looking for love. Come back at 10:00 or 11:00 a.m., and your tough tom may be a pushover.

The same logic applies to later in the season. Most spring turkey seasons are timed to begin after the majority of hens have mated. As the season wears on, flocks become smaller and smaller. Those older, dominant birds suddenly may find themselves alone. Meanwhile, with a good many early-season hunters having tagged out or given up, you may also find yourself alone.

## Hung-Up

Categories of bad birds are not mutually exclusive. For example, birds hang up—refuse to come all the way into range—for various reasons. One of the most common is being henned up, which we addressed above. There are numerous other reasons. Perhaps the bird is call shy (yes, turkeys do get call shy). Maybe there's an obstacle in the way. Or maybe he's just not in the right mood.

My first Maine turkey was one of my more memorable. I first heard him from a long way off and raced to close the distance. I ran out of what I felt was enough cover about 200 yards short of the bird. I could see him, strutting for a hen in a field, across an ankle-deep swamp on

the other side of a barbed wire fence, and uphill. I knew the situation strongly favored the bird, but I also knew I had no other options and therefore little to lose. I called, and he came. I guess he was in the right mood.

One of the best ways to overcome a hung-up bird is to avoid creating one. If you are familiar with the lay of the land, as you should be, don't set up with an obstacle between you and the turkey. Obstacles include fences, water, thick brush, or anything that might give a turkey cause to hesitate. I've seen turkeys totally confounded by a 3-foot-high fence, and deadfall trees might as well be the Great Wall of China.

Another way to take on a hung-up bird is to do a diagnosis—take his temperature. As was discussed briefly in chapter four, first see how he reacts to your calling. Then adjust as needed. If he is clearly answering your call, you can keep calling. If, on the other hand, he seems indifferent, you may want to ease up or cease altogether. In fact, sometimes shutting up will get his attention like nothing else. It takes great patience and composure, but it does work. You can also switch from calling to scratching in the leaves, which can be deadly effective on hung-up birds.

A somewhat common scenario is a bird who's hung up in a strut zone. He continues to gobble and strut back and forth along a fairly consistent path. He may do this for fifteen minutes, or he may strut for an hour or more. If there's enough cover, and you have enough time, you can sometimes close the distance incrementally. Wait until he gets to the far end of his strut zone, then move forward a few yards. Wait as he turns and comes back, then sneak up a few more yards each time he turns and struts away. You don't necessarily have to get within range of his strut zone. Sometimes just getting inside his confidence zone will be enough to make him break and come the rest of the way.

This is where a pair of hunters can really be effective. As described in chapter nine, the shooter remains in position while the caller moves directly away from the tom. The theory is that the gobbler will think the hen is moving away, and he will advance. Since he's so focused on catching up with that hen, he won't be paying any attention to the shooter.

This tactic works best with two experienced hunters, and safety is paramount. As the caller moves out of sight of the shooter, the only clue to the caller's location is his calling. If your fellow hunter decides he doesn't have a shot, you will need a signal from him (worked out beforehand) that it's safe to return to where he's set up.

## Under Pressure

I learned to hunt turkeys, and still do most of my hunting, on land that is open to the public. That means with little exception I'm hunting pressured birds. I've also learned over the last two-and-a-half

decades that being successful means beating the competition, which includes both pressured turkeys and other hunters.

One tactic that has served me well is to hunt late; one example is late morning. Everybody wants to be in the woods at dawn, especially on opening day. You can't blame them. That's when the birds are most vocal and seemingly most vulnerable. However, it doesn't take much pressure to shut things down. The sun comes up, the woods get quiet, and within an hour or two most hunters leave the woods.

The birds are still there, however, and in some cases can actually be more vulnerable. I've observed a phenomenon at this time of the season that I call the "shuffle." Once all the hens in a particular area have been bred, a dominant tom will sometimes leave his home turf and strike out in search of more. Seemingly overnight, longbeards begin showing up in areas they haven't been all spring—sometimes leaving unhuntable private land for huntable public land. They're eager to mate, and they're on unfamiliar ground, which makes them doubly vulnerable.

## Get Back

One of the most obvious ways to avoid hunting pressure is to avoid the most obvious birds. It took me a while to learn this, partly because of naivete but mostly due to my own stubbornness. Scouting from the front seat of my truck, I'd find a bird, study his habits, stake my claim, and assume because I'd been watching him every day that he was mine. Come opening day, I'd quickly learn he "belonged" to a half-dozen other hunters as well.

I still do a lot of preseason (and in-season) scouting from the truck, but when the competition gets tough, I can always fall back on what I learned from those early morning triangulation sessions (chapter five).

## Have Options

This applies to any birds, as discussed in chapter six, but it's especially important when hunting pressured birds to have several options. You may not be the only one willing to go the extra mile to find an unpressured bird. Even exclusive access to an area is no guarantee you won't be interfered with. I've had hunts blown up by dogs, bobcats, cows—you name it. You may have your birds patterned to the minute, but the first time they get busted, their routine changes.

Don't put all your turkey eggs in one basket. Try to locate as many different gobblers on as many different parcels as possible. This way when something goes wrong, you'll have options. Also, scout at odd times of the day. Most hunters will be scouting birds at dawn and dusk and will hunt where they see birds at those times. But turkeys travel considerable distances over the course of a day; by 10:00 or 11:00 a.m. they could be miles from the roost. If you know they're coming, get there ahead of them, and you'll probably have them to yourself.

## Dare to Be Different

Sometimes success with tough toms is as simple as doing something the other hunters aren't. One example mentioned earlier is to hunt late. By mid- to late morning, most hunters are gone. I've also noticed in areas with fields that most hunters set up along the field edges. By going a quarter mile back into the woods, I can sometimes work a bird without interference, for a while.

I've also applied this philosophy to my calling. Despite what some of my peers say, I firmly believe that birds can become call shy. If everyone's walking around the woods doing loud plain yelps, birds become conditioned to it and are less eager to approach.

When hunting public land, I'll often use a much more subtle calling scenario. I may still call a lot, but I use more soft purrs and scratching in the leaves to simulate contentedly feeding turkeys. If that doesn't work, I'll set out my decoys and won't make a sound.

Speaking of decoys, hunting pressured birds sometimes calls for radically different tactics, several of which were mentioned in previous chapters. Most hunters use between one and three decoys. Coaxing a henned-up tom with a big harem may require twice that number or even more. A strutting-tom decoy will sometimes work when nothing else does. It could even provide cover for you to move closer to your quarry.

You can apply the "dare to be different" philosophy to the weapon you choose. The reason there are so many hunters where I live is that there are so many people, and those people live in developed areas. So do turkeys. They've adapted quite well to living around the trappings of humans in my part of the world. Many of these suburban birds go largely unhunted, unless and until a bowhunter comes along. One of my best birds came from a small parcel of state-

owned land that was too close to houses to discharge a firearm—but not a bow.

## The Old Guard

The mid-2000s were an interesting period for turkey hunters. At first I thought maybe it was just my bad luck, but it seemed too much of a coincidence to find tough toms everywhere I went, from New England to Florida, the Gulf Coast to Texas, and throughout the Midwest. Then I started comparing notes with other turkey hunters at conventions and trade shows, and their stories were the same: Birds just refused to come to the call. But we had another thing in common; when we did get a bird, it was usually a good one.

The problem, I surmised, was a shortage of young birds. Those wonderful two-year-olds that make you feel like a turkey hunter—movie stars, as Will Primos calls them— were missing in action. Weather was certainly a factor in some areas. The Northeast had experienced four consecutive years of cold, wet weather right at hatching time. Consequently, we were left with old birds to hunt.

■ I took this bird on a small parcel of state land where no gun hunter could go. It ended up being the state record by bow.

■ Sometimes in order to kill a tough old limbhanger, you have to think outside the box and hunt outside the book.

Now, turkeys may not be the wisest birds in the woods, but they learn from experience. And I firmly believe they learn to avoid hunters and calling. It's kind of like a mature buck who's learned he doesn't really need to do much chasing. When the girls are ready, they'll come to him. He will not go to a call and often will go away from one.

These old birds are uncallable but not unkillable. You just need to employ different tactics. The most reliable method is ambush. Scout your bird extensively, and set up where he travels regularly. Leave the calls and the decoys at home. Be patient and silent. I once killed an old limbhanger in Alabama by setting up on the route he traveled to reach his evening roost. I sat down at 2:30 in the afternoon, yelped on a slate three times every hour, and finally pulled the trigger at 6:45 p.m.

There is another effective tactic for bad birds that should at least be mentioned. Though perfectly legal and well within the ethical bounds of fair chase, it is considered by some to be a serious breech of safety. As my old pal George Mayfield so succinctly says, "If you can't call 'em, crawl 'em." As far as how you go about it, I'll leave that up to you. I will, however, advise you that safety must be foremost in your mind at all times. Don't even think about trying this on public ground, and thorough consideration should be given even when hunting on private ground where you have exclusive privileges.

Tough toms, bad birds, call them what you will. They defy the rules of fair play; they test our wits and our mettle. But they also teach us. Each loss makes us wiser, and as a friend once told me when referring to challenging birds, "He can beat me a dozen times. I only have to win once."

■ If the birds simply refuse to come to a call, you may be better off putting it away and merely waiting them out.

# CHAPTER ELEVEN

# Specialties: Bowhunting and Fall Hunting

## Bowhunting

I firmly contend that turkeys were put on this earth to be killed with a shotgun, and bowhunting them is an unnatural act. Having said that, I freely admit that I started flinging arrows at them over a decade ago and still spend a considerable amount of every spring trying to *do it the hard way.* I'm no longer the oddball. Bowhunting in general has become immensely popular. Not surprisingly, this meteoric rise in interest has spilled over from big game into turkey hunting.

Whether it's archers taking up turkey hunting or turkey hunters taking up archery, members of both groups are looking for more and greater challenges. No matter how you do it, archery represents turkey hunting's ultimate challenge.

■ **Whatever type of bow you choose, select one you are comfortable and confident with and can shoot well.**

Still, you can tilt the odds decidedly in your favor by following some general guidelines.

## Technique

Techniques for bowhunting turkeys are largely the same as for gunning them, up to a point. You still need to locate the birds, then call them into range. It is at that point

that the two styles diverge immensely. The shotgunner needs only to pull the trigger. The bowhunter must draw, aim, and shoot—all in close proximity to some of the sharpest eyes in the animal kingdom—and be able to hit an area roughly the size of a baseball with a single projectile. Difficult yes, but not impossible.

The first great impediment is drawing your bow. They're not so good on stationary objects, but a turkey's ability to detect movement is acute. I swear I've had birds bust me because they saw me blink. The

best remedy for a bowhunter is to hunt from a blind, where you can move undetected. Portable pop-up blinds are ideal, as they offer both concealment and at least some measure of mobility. In a pinch you can fashion a makeshift blind of natural material or loose camo cloth, though that offers a bit less concealment and commits you to one location.

While their eyesight is keen and their ability to avoid predators acute, turkeys aren't the brightest of woodland creatures. Occasionally, they see movement

■ Decoys help take the turkey's attention away from the shooter and position the bird for a better shot angle.

■ The crossbow just might be the ultimate turkey-hunting weapon. It offers all the up-close thrills of bowhunting without the excessive burden of having to draw at ultraclose range.

and simply don't react. It's a very-low-percentage option, but you can sometimes even kill birds "running and gunning" with no more cover than a 3-D leafy suit. Naturally, the more you use existing cover, such as trees, bushes, and terrain, the better your odds.

Decoys are also strongly recommended. First, they can often make the difference in luring a reluctant tom those all-important final few yards. More importantly for the bowhunter, they focus the bird's attention and keen eyesight away from you. They can also be helpful in

positioning a bird for the shot—something the gun hunter is less concerned with.

## Equipment

### Bows

If you already bowhunt, you're in luck because you can use largely the same archery equipment you use for deer hunting. This is particularly helpful in the fall, when you can hunt both. If, on the other hand, you're a turkey hunter switching to archery and you plan on buying a bow just for turkeys, a compound bow is your best option. Compounds offer the mechanical advantage of let-off, which allows you to hold your bow at full draw for a longer duration. They're also easier to learn to shoot. If you already have a recurve or longbow and are proficient, that's fine. But these are not a good choice for the beginning bowhunter. An even better option, where legal, is the crossbow. It offers an even greater advantage as it is mechanically held at full draw. In the case of both recurves and compounds, lighter draw weights are advantageous because they're easier to pull and hold.

Turkeys are also adept at detecting color. Make sure your bow has no shiny or brightly colored hardware visible. Anything like a sight screw or a limb bolt that could reflect sunlight should be camouflaged. Also, arrow fletching should be either drab colored or concealed. Turkeys will easily pick out bright colors such as yellow, orange, or chartreuse; and red and white are dangerous when turkey hunting as other hunters could mistake them for a gobbler's head.

■ Because energy loss is not a concern, arrow pass-through is not desirable, and a large wound channel is important, mechanical or expandable broadheads offer a decided advantage.

## Broadheads

Broadheads work by cutting arteries, veins, and organs, which results in significant blood loss and organ malfunction (see following sidebar). The broadhead-arrow combination may also break bones and inflict severe muscle damage that prevents or significantly hinders an animal's escape. While immobilizing a turkey with the shot is preferable, it's not always possible and certainly not necessary to bag your bird, or reduce the animal to possession.

Both fixed and mechanical heads will effectively kill a turkey with proper shot placement. However, those with larger cutting diameters are more effective. Their larger size helps compensate for a smaller vital area, and the larger surface area will reduce the possibility of complete pass-through—something you don't want when turkey hunting. Both those reasons are why I give mechanical heads the edge for turkeys.

Another option is the so-called guillotine heads. They have long fixed blades and ridiculously large cutting diameters. The idea is that you shoot at the bird's head knowing there's a high probability at least one of the blades will make contact, breaking the neck and sometimes lopping the head clean off. They're extremely effective on impact. One downside is that they require specialized arrows—extra long with 7- or 8-inch extreme helical feather fletching. Another is that trajectory is reliable only to 15 or 20 yards.

## Recovery

Turkeys are tough. The first step toward recovering the bird is discussed above—making a lethal shot. The rest involves keeping your head and following a few simple steps.

If the bird is down within sight and appears to be having difficulty escaping, proceed quickly, but in a controlled manner, to the bird. If it is still moving, place your foot on the neck or head to hold the bird securely until it expires. Always be mindful of your broadhead, too, as it may still be inside the bird or protruding from the turkey's body.

If the bird runs or flies quickly away, it is often better to wait for it to bleed out and expire before pursuing it. There are cases where it is better to pursue immediately, but that becomes a judgment call best made based on experience.

Should the bird manage to escape, watch it until it goes out of sight. Take a bearing on its direction of travel. Pick out a landmark at the last place you saw it, then wait. How long you should wait can depend on several things, including how accurate you believe your shot was. Often, a badly hit bird will only travel a short distance before seeking cover.

Remember, the longer you let it lie, the better your chances of recovering it. If it is dead, it won't be going anywhere. If it's not, it could be flushed and may then run away to where you will not recover it.

After you have determined the necessary waiting period has passed, begin

## SHOT PLACEMENT

### Where to Shoot a Turkey

The ultimate goal of arrow placement is to disrupt an animal's circulatory, neurological, muscular, or skeletal systems so that the animal is immobilized or disabled to the point where it cannot escape. To accomplish this on a turkey, the archer should try to hit one of three primary aiming spots.

The head-neck-spine area contains the turkey's primary neurological systems. It's a largely vertical target zone. A hit here will typically immobilize the bird, often killing it instantly.

The vital organs (heart, lung, liver) occupy an area about the size of a man's fist and also contain the majority of a turkey's blood. This is a more horizontal target zone. Unless the broadhead also strikes bone, a turkey hit here will often travel some distance before succumbing to the injury.

Turkeys have two modes of escape, running or flying. In order to fly, they must first use their powerful legs to launch into the air. A shot that breaks one or both upper legs will significantly impede the bird's ability to escape.

### Where to Aim

Where you should aim will depend on the turkey's orientation and posture. The broadside shot is ideal because it presents all three primary aiming spots. The vital organs lie inside the upper half of the folded wing. On a bird that is standing upright, aim for the row of bronze-colored feathers (the wing coverts) toward the top of the wing. A shot that is too low will still break one or both legs. A shot that is too high will break the spine.

On a strutting tom, move your point of aim forward and up to the leading edge of the coverts. You can find it by following a horizontal line from the base of the tail feathers forward to the base of the featherless neck. Aim where this line intersects a vertical line up from the legs.

A quartering-away shot is less desirable but can still reach the vital organs. You just need to move your point of aim back from where you'd aim on a broadside shot. How far back depends on the angle. Just visualize both the entry and exit locations, as you would with a deer.

The quartering-to and straight-on positions are less desirable still. They can be lethal body shots but present a smaller vital area. Furthermore, the arrow must first pass through dense feathers, meat, and breastbone before reaching the vitals.

Straight on, aim for the center of the chest—left to right and roughly a third of the way down between the top of the head and the bottom of the body.

While the rear end is a shot no ethical bowhunter would take at any other animal, it actually provides several good options for a turkey hunter. When a tom is strutting, the tail feathers are raised and fanned. The central junction of these feathers, at the base of the tail, offers an ideal bulls-eye. The arrow will travel through the body, passing through the vital organs and possibly breaking the spine. With the tail feathers up and fanned, this also affords the hunter an opportunity to draw the bow undetected. If the tom has relaxed and lowered his tail feathers, the head/neck aiming spot may then become a target. From the rear, the full length of the spine is also available and is a quick-kill target preferred by many experienced turkey hunters.

searching in the direction the turkey went. A fatally hit turkey will often travel in a straight line and seek the first available cover. Move slowly and quietly along, "hunting" for the bird, paying particular attention to brush piles, thickets, and other small, thick places where it could hide. A turkey may even enter water to hide under embankments. Look hard, and get help if necessary.

## Fall Hunting

Spring is mating season, when you try to exploit a gobbler's amorous Achilles heel by imitating a lovesick hen. In the fall you're relying more on the turkey's gregarious nature. Furthermore, most fall seasons are for either sex. Though fall birds are less inclined to come to a call, they will, especially if you give them a reason.

The prototypical technique for fall turkey hunting is fairly straightforward and simple. You locate a flock of birds, scatter them, then call them back. The effectiveness of this method, however, can depend on several variables, including flock composition and whether or not you get a good break.

Brood flocks consisting of hens and nearly adult poults are the most susceptible. These young birds have likely never been apart from their mother or siblings for any length of time, and when you bust 'em up, they're eager to get back together. They'll often begin regrouping within fifteen or twenty minutes.

Jakes are somewhat indifferent about companionship and may take several hours to regroup. And adult toms are downright antisocial. When separated from their peers, it may take them several days to get back together.

In any case you need a good break. Get as close to the birds as you can (or let them get close to you) before you rush at them, screaming like a banshee. If you frighten the birds and they all escape in more or less the same direction, it's far more difficult to predict where they'll regroup, but

■ In most states fall hunting is for either sex, which increases your odds for success and provides a great opportunity to break in a young hunter.

it probably won't be anywhere near you. If, on the other hand, you scatter the birds in different directions, there's a very good chance they'll reconvene at or near the break point, which is what you want.

If you get a bad break, you're better off giving up and locating another flock. Subsequent breaks on the same flock are less productive, as the birds are now more frightened and closemouthed. Timing can also be important when using this method. Turkeys are much more inclined to regroup when scattered early in the day.

Assuming you get a good break, move to the position you last saw the flock, set

yourself up, wait ten to fifteen minutes, and begin calling. By then you may already be hearing the *kee-kee*s or lost hen yelps of lonely birds looking for their running mates. As far as calling, all you really have to do is pay attention to what you hear and mimic it.

## Fall Calls

The most popular fall calls are the *kee-kee*, the *kee-kee-run*, and the lost hen yelp. The *kee-kee* is a high-pitched whistle made by the young birds. Like a teenager whose voice cracks, they sometimes lapse from *kee-kee*s into yelps, which is termed the *kee-kee-run.* Lonesome hens or brood hens trying to reassemble their young will sometimes utter eight to ten even-pitched yelps. Again, whatever you hear, you duplicate. A nonvocalization that sometimes works alone or in conjunction with calls is scratching in the leaves to simulate the sound of feeding turkeys.

## Spot-and-Stalk

Scattering the flock is by no means the only method for hunting fall turkeys. You can also spot and stalk them. You'll cover a lot more ground if you can drive the roads and look for flocks in open fields. Good areas include fields of recently cut corn, recently plowed ground, or recently spread manure. Scattering a flock from a field is usually a losing proposition (unless you can team up with another hunter), and you don't actually stalk the birds either—that would be dangerous. Instead, try to determine in which direction the flock is headed, then sneak around and set up ahead of them. If they move by you into the woods, you can revert to scattering. This method is also a good fallback plan later in the morning, if scattering fails to produce in the early a.m.

## Positioning

Yet another fall hunting method involves merely setting up along a regular travel route and waiting the birds out—ambushing. Turkeys tend to be very habitual in the fall—roosting in the same trees and moving to and from the same feeding areas.

### FINDING THEM

One of the best ways to find turkeys in the fall is to find a food source. Turkeys are very dependent on and faithful to concentrated sources of preferred fall foods. In forested areas this generally means acorns and beechnuts. In agricultural areas it may mean waste grain like corn, soybeans, or wheat. Transition zones or old fields are also good places to look, as birds will often use them to forage on abundant, soft mast, such as raspberries, barberries, and multiflora roses.

You should also try to find a roost site. Watching and listening, particularly at dawn and dusk, is a good way to locate turkeys close to the roost. Fall turkeys make a lot of noise, especially early in the morning. Hens and poults do a lot of yelping and kee-keeing, and jakes especially will sometimes gobble at this time of year. An accumulation of droppings, feathers, and scratching under tall trees is also a good indication of a roost.

Much as you would in the spring, sneak in before light and set up close to a roost, between the roost and a feeding area (as opposed to directly under the roost).

You can sometimes increase the effectiveness of this method by busting the roost just after the birds have flown up. The key is to scatter, not scare. The birds will be apart all night and will be particularly eager to regroup at first light the next morning. Whether you bust the roost or not, it's still a good place to end the day. Birds may happen by on their way to roost.

■ Turkeys tend to be quite regular with their daily routine in the fall. This makes scouting particularly important.

If not, just sit and listen. If you hear them flying up, you'll know where to begin the next morning. If you see birds, pay particular attention to the route they take going to the roost, as they'll often follow the reverse route the next morning.

## Equipment

In the fall you'll be using roughly the same turkey-hunting equipment as in the spring. You'll need camouflage from head to toe, including gloves, boots, and a face mask or face paint. However, you may want to change the particular pattern you wear if your spring camo has a lot of green. By the latter part of October, at least in northern areas, the leaves have dropped, and woods are tinted with drabber grays and browns.

You can also use decoys in much the same way as you would in the spring. They don't seem to be as important for fall hunting, but they can help in certain instances, particularly when you're restricted to a blind. In most cases one decoy is all you'll need. Remember to exercise extreme caution, as even hen decoys could attract the attention of other hunters. Make sure you have a solid backstop. You may also want to hang an orange ribbon nearby, just to alert other hunters to your presence.

## Safety/Ethics/Responsibility

Safety should always be foremost on your mind while turkey hunting, particularly in the fall. You are fully camouflaged, hidden, and imitating the sound of your intended game, as are other hunters in the woods. This increases the potential for an accident. Ethics and responsibility should also be high on your list of considerations. In addition to turkey hunters, you may also be sharing the woods with deer and bird hunters, and knowing proper safety and hunting etiquette can go a long way toward making everyone's hunt safer and more enjoyable.

■ It is said that the toughest turkey to kill is a mature longbeard in the fall. Add archery tackle to the mix, and you just might have turkey hunting's ultimate challenge.

---

### TARGETING TOMS

A mature gobbler is the most difficult turkey to kill in the fall. Add the constraint of archery tackle, and you have a daunting challenge indeed. Hunting a mature tom is, in many ways, like hunting a mature buck outside the rut. Your best odds for success lie in being where the turkey wants to go anyway. Scout as much as you can, and observe where you see gobblers during various times of day. If you can detect a routine, that will also be helpful. Your calling must also be more conservative, consisting of just a few clucks or yelps. Gobblers do yelp and cluck, though their calls are deeper, coarser, and more drawn out than those of hens. If you're trying to call them, yelp or cluck once or twice. Then shut up and wait. If they want to come, they will. If not, additional calling will likely do more harm than good.

# CHAPTER TWELVE

# Ethics and Safety

**M**ost of the information provided to this point is intended to make your hunting experience a positive one. A successful hunt goes a long way toward that end, but you don't necessarily need to fill your tag to have had a good hunt or to be successful. For some, perhaps many, it is everything that went into the experience

■ Teach your children. If we instill a sense of safety and ethics in young hunters, it will become ingrained in them and the sport and provide a more positive experience for future generations of hunters.

that ultimately determines whether it is one you'll long remember—or would just as soon forget. Often the deciding factor is how we interact with our fellow sportsmen.

## Ethics

I tell the students in my hunter-safety classes that ethics is what you do when no one else is looking. We should all follow the law, but ethics transcends what's written in the law books. It involves the gray areas, where there may not be any specific rules or guidelines, but we still know the difference between right and wrong. In many ways it boils down to being respectful toward the game we pursue, the people upon whose land we hunt, and those we share that land with, including other hunters and nonhunters.

Doug Howlett, who wrote the foreword to this book, provides a good example. "I was fall turkey hunting with a large group of hunters. We spotted two flocks of turkeys in the same field and executed two perfect flushes. Several birds were shot on the break. The hunters who had yet to shoot then set up and killed a few more on the call back. All told, we took seven turkeys from two flocks of about fifteen to twenty birds each.

"After celebrating our success, I asked the landowner, with whom I was hunting, if he would go back in on those flocks again later in the season. Though it would have been perfectly legal, he told me they wouldn't hunt those turkeys anymore

that fall. We'd all taken our share, and he didn't want to do anything that might risk the future potential for turkeys on that property." That is an excellent example of respecting the resource.

As good hunting grounds become increasingly scarce, it is even more important to keep in mind how the nonhunting public views our actions. I have a friend, Jon, who works at a ski area that also has a year-round restaurant. Turkeys have recently settled into the area, and the first few springs a big tom made quite a spectacle of himself, strutting across the verdant slopes in plain view of all the ski-area workers and restaurant visitors.

As head of maintenance, Jon also has permission to hunt the ski area. But he refused to hunt that particular bird. His reasoning was that if he killed the bird, it would be quite obvious to the nonhunters who work and visit the area what had happened, and it could leave them with a bad impression of hunters. I wonder how many of us would make that sacrifice, for that reason.

### Ethics and Etiquette

You've scouted a flock of birds all spring. You know where they roost, where they fly down, and where they go first thing in the morning to strut and feed. You sleep fitfully the night before opening day, going over your mental checklist a thousand times to make sure you haven't forgotten anything, and hoping all will go well in the morning.

You wake far too early, gulp down a quick breakfast, jump in the truck, and you're off. As you round the last corner, your headlights reflect off another vehicle. Someone else is already there. What should you do, and perhaps more important, what will you do?

*There's a thousand acres here—plenty of room for a couple of guys,* you rationalize.

## THE RESPONSIBLE TURKEY HUNTER'S CODE OF ETHICS

As a responsible turkey hunter, I will
- not let peer pressure or the excitement of the hunt cloud my judgment;
- learn and practice safe hunting techniques;
- hunt the wild turkey fairly;
- know the capabilities and limitations of my gun or bow and use it safely;
- obey and support all wildlife laws and report all violations;
- respect the land and the landowner and always obtain permission before hunting;
- avoid knowingly interfering with another hunter and respect the right of others to lawfully share the out-of-doors;
- value the hunting experience and appreciate the beauty of the wild turkey;
- positively identify my target as a legal bird and insist on a good shot;
- and share responsible turkey hunting with others and work for wild turkey conservation.

That may be true, and you could probably even make a good, ethical argument for hunting there. Somewhere in the back of your mind, though, don't you feel just a little uneasy?

A big component of ethics is etiquette—how we treat our fellow hunters. Here again, a lot of it is common sense and common courtesy. For those of you new to the sport, there are also some general guidelines.

In the above scenario the unwritten rule is simple: The first guy there gets the spot—period. By entering the same block of woods as another hunter, you not only increase the odds of messing up the hunt, but you also put yourself and the other guy at risk. If you did your homework, you should have other options. Being a guide, I'm especially sensitive to this and always yield when someone gets there ahead of me, which doesn't happen very often. Keep an eye out for decoys, too, and react to them the same way you do to posted signs—keep away.

Sometimes having multiple hunters in the same area is unavoidable. Perhaps you each entered from different access points, or the other hunter came in after you. Regardless of how it happened, you may encounter a situation where you come upon another hunter in the process of working a bird. He calls and the bird answers, but it's not moving in his direction, and it's closer to you. What will you do?

Here again, the answer is simple. Leave. Never, ever move in on a bird

■ **Whether you hear calling or not, never move in too close or too fast on a gobbling tom. Stop some distance away and listen for other hunters nearby.**

that someone else is calling. At best, you might screw up his hunt. At worst, someone could get shot. A gobbler will often make his final approach to a calling hunter silently. The hunter is looking for movement—any movement. Though it should never happen, you could be mistaken for a turkey.

You could also unknowingly place yourself in the path of a load of No. 4s if a turkey comes between you and the other hunter. This happened to me several years ago when another hunter, a guide no less, moved in on two gobblers I was calling.

Had he not given two soft clucks on a box call, I never would have known he was there. I passed up an easy shot and got a severe tongue lashing for "moving in on his bird" for my troubles.

Making other hunters aware of your presence is always good practice. When moving through the woods, display some orange for your own safety and out of consideration for other hunters. When sitting, an occasional yelp will establish a wall of sound around you. Whether he thinks you're turkey or human, no knowledgeable hunter will approach.

Avoid crowded areas. Some places just seem to draw the crowds, and the more turkey hunters present, the greater the chance for an accident. There may be a lot of birds there, but more likely than not you'll end up getting frustrated. Just as you get set up and start to call, some nimrod will bumble in and blow it for you. Besides, resident birds in pressured areas become call shy quickly.

When hunting around fields, always approach slowly and glass the field before stepping into the open. Otherwise you could ruin an opportunity for yourself or someone else who's been patiently sitting and calling for hours. More than once I've had inattentive hunters stumble into a field and spook birds I was working. What's even more surprising? They usually don't even realize it.

■ Regardless of your choice of weapon, make sure you practice and become proficient with it in order to make a quick, clean kill.

---

## TEN COMMANDMENTS OF FIREARM SAFETY

1. Treat every firearm with the same respect due a loaded firearm.
2. Control the direction of your firearm's muzzle.
3. Be sure of your target and what is beyond it.
4. Be sure the barrel and action are clear of obstructions.
5. Unload firearms when not in use.
6. Never point a firearm at anything you do not want to shoot.
7. Never climb a fence or tree, or jump a ditch or log, with a loaded firearm.
8. Never shoot a bullet at a flat, hard surface or water.
9. Store firearms and ammunition separately.
10. Avoid alcoholic beverages or other mood-altering drugs before or while shooting.

---

As ethical, responsible sportsmen, we have certain behaviors expected of us. We need to learn and follow the written as well as the unwritten rules. We need to demonstrate respect for the animals we hunt, the land we hunt on and its owners, and those we share the woods with—be they hunters or not.

The above are examples of the types of situations we face each spring and fall that measure our personal hunting ethics. Making the right decisions is critical for the perpetuation of healthy game populations and the protection of hunting. We need to be respectful of those who don't hunt as well as those who do, in order to ensure that everyone has a safe and enjoyable experience in the woods. Demograph ics show that many who don't hunt aren't necessarily opposed to others doing it, but it only takes one transgression to sway them over to the other side.

## Safety

Turkey hunting is dangerous. How many times have you heard that phrase? In truth, it can be but only when participants fail to follow the rules and the standard safety practices. According to the National Wild Turkey Federation, you're more likely to be injured playing volleyball. Statistically, turkey hunting is four times safer than Ping-Pong, and you are fifty times more likely to take a trip to the emergency room if you play golf. You can increase those odds in your favor exponentially if you follow a few common-sense guidelines.

## Basics

With the exception of a few who were grandfathered, most hunters today had to take a hunter-safety class in order to get their first hunting license. The first thing every one of us is taught in that class is the ten commandments of gun safety. By now they should be ingrained in your head, second nature. All apply to turkey hunting, but a couple really stand out. Turkey-hunting injuries, for the most part, can be lumped into two categories: self-inflicted and mistaken-as-game. Both are preventable if you follow a few simple rules.

*Treat every firearm with the same respect due a loaded firearm.* That one incorporates several of the others: control the direction of your firearm's muzzle; be sure the barrel and action are clear of obstructions; unload your gun when it's not in use, but never assume it's unloaded; and never climb a fence or tree, or jump a ditch or log, with a loaded firearm. Simple, straightforward, and common sense; yet every year people forget. They get lax or impatient, and somebody gets hurt.

*Be sure of your target and what lies beyond it.* There really is no excuse for a mistaken-as-game accident. Turkeys don't look like hunters. They don't dress in camo, and they don't carry guns. Unless you are absolutely, positively, 100 percent certain it's a turkey (a living, breathing turkey, not a decoy), you shouldn't even be aiming at it.

This rule also addresses a third common cause of injury. Occasionally, someone is hit by stray pellets from another hunter who is legitimately shooting at a turkey. In many cases it is the victim's fault for moving in or trying to sneak up on a bird that someone else is calling. You can never be too careful about identifying your target and beyond.

## Defensive Hunting

It would be great if we could all just hit the woods and do as we please. But unless you have exclusive access to a piece of property, and you are certain you're the only one hunting it, you can't. In addition to doing all you can to prevent an injury, there's much you can do to prevent being the victim of one. That involves thinking and hunting defensively. What follows are a few tips toward that end.

*Find a safe backstop.* When calling, try to sit against a stump, blowdown, tree trunk, or rock that is wider than your shoulders and higher than your head. This will at least protect your blind side. Furthermore, you're more likely to spot another hunter moving to the front or side than from behind.

*Be still.* You should do this anyway. You never know when a turkey might slip in silently, and if it catches you moving, the game is over. It's best not to move, wave, or make turkey sounds to alert another hunter of your presence. Instead, remain still and speak in a loud, clear voice to announce your position.

*Use common sense when choosing clothing.* Never wear anything that is red, white, blue, or black. These are the colors of a male turkey, and though it should never happen, you could be mistaken for one. Also, wear dark undershirts and socks and pants long enough to be tucked into boots. If you do wear white undergarments or socks, make sure they're covered up.

*Try to call from open timber rather than thick brush.* This gives you a better view of anything approaching your position, be it turkey or hunter. And by all means, be discreet when imitating the sound of a gobbling turkey. On public land this is a no-no. Even hen calling will sometimes attract other hunters, but gobbling is sure to bring them running.

*Be alert.* If you're a good woodsman, you can sometimes detect the approach of something or someone by watching other game or listening for the alarm cries of blue jays, crows, squirrels, or woodpeckers.

## Hunting with Decoys

Using decoys can be an extremely effective tactic, but it can also increase the potential for an incident. Many of today's decoys are quite realistic. In fact, more hunters are using actual stuffed turkeys as decoys. Though it shouldn't happen, there's always the possibility you could draw fire from unknowing hunters.

There are some steps you can take to minimize the chances. For starters, never transport decoys uncovered. If they fold up, you can tote them in your vest. If you're using larger toms, molded decoys, or stuffers, carry them in a bag, preferably an orange one.

If at all possible, try to set your decoys so that you have a good, open field of view, which will enable you to see anyone or

■ **When calling, it's best to sit against a tree or other solid backstop that is at least as wide as your shoulders.**

anything approaching. As stated above, set up against a solid backstop that is taller than your head and wider than your shoulders, and make sure you have a clear line of vision in front of you.

## Other Dangers

Though firearms safety should always be foremost in the mind of every turkey hunter, far more of us are injured and killed each year by causes not directly related to hunting. For example, the number-one killer of all outdoorsmen is hypothermia—a lowering of the body's temperature due to exposure to the elements. Cold air draws heat away from your body, and that process is accelerated rapidly if you're wet.

That's why you should always dress properly for the conditions. As discussed in chapter three, dress in layers. You can always remove excess clothing, but you can't add it if you don't have it. Wear moisture-wicking base layers and waterproof outer layers if necessary. If you're going to be out for any length of time or far from a road, it's also not a bad idea to carry a small survival kit, which contains at the very least waterproof matches, a knife, a compass, a whistle, a space blanket, a high-energy snack, and a bottle of water.

There are also all sorts of creepy-crawly things out there that you should at least be aware of. Some are merely a nuisance, while others can be potentially life threatening.

Snakes don't bother me, but they do worry some folks. If you're among them, you should at least be aware of which ones could harm you, what they look like, and where they live. Get a field guide or go online.

Cottonmouths or water moccasins range from the South Atlantic, Gulf, and lower Midwestern states to eastern Texas and Oklahoma. As

■ For the most part, snakes won't bother you if you don't bother them. Still, it's a good idea to keep an eye out for them as you make your way through the turkey woods.

their name implies, these large black snakes prefer low, wetland areas. They are venomous and very aggressive. Also in the same genus is the copperhead. Its range extends farther north into southern New England and west across southern Ohio, Indiana, Illinois, Iowa, and eastern Nebraska. It is smaller and well camouflaged, and more docile, and it prefers upland areas.

There are more than a dozen species of rattlesnakes, some of which occur just about everywhere except New England, the Lake states and the Pacific Northwest. All are venomous, but like most snakes, they will go out of their way to avoid humans if given the chance.

I don't mind spiders too much either, so long as they don't bother me. Still, there are a dozen or so that are venomous and a few you should be aware of. Perhaps the most insidious is the brown recluse or fiddleback spider. At less than an inch long, this rather nondescript little devil packs quite a wallop. In addition to being very painful, its bite can cause significant cutaneous injury, with tissue loss and necrosis. Smaller still, the tiny black widow can inflict a bite that's painful and potentially fatal, especially to the young and elderly. Both the brown recluse and the black widow inhabit the woodpiles and fallen trees that turkey hunters so love to lean against.

Another closely related arachnid is the scorpion. They seem more menacing (at least to me), but their sting—said to be like that of a wasp—is rarely serious. Like a bee sting or spider bite, however, it can cause anaphylactic shock (a severe allergic reaction). Fortunately, scorpions aren't all that common, limited primary to the arid Southwest, though they do favor the same woodpiles and debris turkey hunters love to nestle into.

Far more outdoorsmen are probably afflicted by the spider's distant eight-legged cousins, the ticks. They can spread such diseases as Rocky Mountain spotted fever, babesiosis, erlichiosis, and Lyme disease. Typically, you shouldn't have to worry about them if you check yourself every day after leaving the field. If in doubt, see your physician.

Mosquitoes and blackflies are generally more of an annoyance than anything, though mosquitoes are usually to blame for localized outbreaks of West Nile virus, which can be fatal.

Fear not. If you spend enough time in the woods, you're likely to encounter a good many of the creatures and situations described above. That may sound a bit intimidating at first. But bear in mind that with few exceptions you will escape with little more than a bad mood. Spiders and scorpions, snakes and slobs, I've encountered them all and ended up none the worse for the wear. I still greet each spring and yearn for the woods with the same zeal as when I first started my life as a turkey hunter.

# CHAPTER THIRTEEN

# Care and Handling

I loathe preparing my birds for cooking. It's not so much the process of plucking, skinning, and dismembering that I mind. What bothers me is the idea of converting such a magnificent bird into something as utilitarian as table fare. It's like cutting up an original Rembrandt for a school project. I'd mount every one if I could afford it—just to honor the bird. Instead, I save what I can and eat the rest. The process begins the moment you pull the trigger, sometimes even before.

One of my first sponsored hunts was with Brad Harris, then of Lohman Game Calls, and fellow writer Jim Casada. I spotted a pair of longbeards across an open field, and after a lengthy bout of calling against the high Kansas winds, Brad was able to lure both within range. I rolled one, but he quickly righted himself and commenced beating a hasty retreat.

I sprung to my feet and hit the ground running, at the same time cycling another round into the 3½-inch chamber of my Mossberg 835 Ulti-Mag. I quickly regained gun range on the stunned bird, but instead of simply throwing a pattern of shot at center of mass, I took careful aim at the bird's head—not wanting to body shoot him.

That may work fine on a bird that's standing still, but it's often less effective when the bird is on a dead run (if you'll pardon the pun). I shot right over the top of him, leaving me with one more shot.

Again I tore off after the bird, soon regained ground, then stopped just long enough to click off the safety and shoulder my gun. At this point, most folks would have seen the error of their ways and thrown lead at the bird. Not me. I again took careful aim and went for a head shot, with similar effectiveness. Since I was now out of ammo, it then became a foot race, which I ultimately won.

Even then, while wrestling the still-very-alive bird as he spurred me and beat me with his wings, I tried my best to keep from tearing him up too badly. Part of it was out of respect, and part was wanting to keep him neat enough for good photos. Silly? Maybe, but that was not the stupidest thing I've done to preserve the integrity of a bird.

Whether you're planning on a full body mount or just want a respectful photo of your trophy, you should decide in advance so you can take proper steps to keep the bird looking as good as possible.

## Hero Shots

Memories of a special hunt can fade over time unless you've done a good job of capturing the moment in pictures. And like the story, those pictures should be something that you're proud to share with others. What follows are a few tips on taking quality hero shots.

## Presentation

First, and perhaps foremost, create a neat, clean scene. Remove any blood from you and your bird. You can use a few moist wipes, even some toilet paper to clean off any blood, especially from the animal's face and your hands and clothing. Smooth out ruffled feathers. Put on your best camos or clean off any mud, dirt, and leaves from you and your trophy. You don't want the photo to look as though you had to wrestle the poor beast to death, even if you did.

Cleaning up the background is just as important. Clutter is very distracting and can ruin an otherwise pleasing photo. It's tempting and easy, and everyone does it, but don't take photos of your turkey in the back of a pickup truck. Also, avoid logo shirts; they look tacky. Move the trophy away from buildings or piles of junk. You want a neutral background with no distracting items. If you're shooting in a field, pay particular attention to the horizon. A skyline cutting through the hunter's head is also very distracting.

Consider safety and ethics. If there's a gun in the photo, make sure the muzzle

■ Granted, your overall objective is reducing a turkey to possession. Still, you should show respect in that process by not tearing the bird up unnecessarily.

is pointing in a safe direction. And don't forget to smile.

## Composition and Position

Composition is another area that can make a huge difference in the quality of your photo. Change camera settings to reduce the depth of field, and reduce distracting backgrounds by putting them

■ Use your trophy shot to preserve the memory of a special hunt. Shoot in similar habitat, wear the same camo, and include your gun, other items, and people that contributed to your success.

out of focus. Avoid shooting down at the subject. Shooting from a low angle helps enhance the animal's size. The best pose for a turkey is either on the ground in front of you or propped on your knee. In either case spread the fan out and make sure the beard is visible. Don't center the shot; try to place the main subject slightly

off to one side. Another trick is to compose the scene so it leads the viewer's eyes from right to left.

### General Photo Tips

Shoot digital. Film is cheap, but disk space is even cheaper. In addition, you can look at the images to make sure you've captured the subject. Take lots of photos, and bracket every shot. This means changing your f-stop one or even two stops above and below your metered level. Try several different poses, and bracket each one.

When you take photos is also important. The intense, direct light of midday will wash out colors. Conversely, low light early and late in the day will always produce a sharper, more colorful image. If you take photos at midday, avoid direct sunlight. Pose the subject in the shade and use a flash. Even if you have sufficient ambient light, using a fill-flash can sometimes help reduce distracting shadows on the face.

Whenever possible, use a tripod. This prevents camera shake from those who punch the shutter, which results in blurred images. When composing the shot on a tripod, make sure the camera is plumb and level, as a canted photo is also distracting.

### Field Dressing

When it comes to field dressing, there are two schools of thought. One recommends cleaning your bird right away. The quicker you remove the animal's entrails, the less chance of spoilage. The other

## FIELD DRESSING A WILD TURKEY

Note: On a bird you suspect may weigh in excess of 20 lbs., you will want to weigh the bird whole, on certified scales.

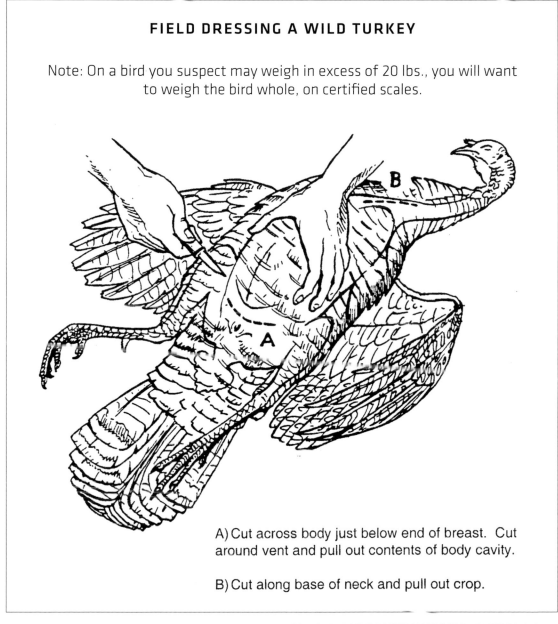

A) Cut across body just below end of breast. Cut around vent and pull out contents of body cavity.

B) Cut along base of neck and pull out crop.

suggests waiting; the primary reason here is weight. Everyone likes to know what his bird weighs, and weight contributes to the overall score. Turkeys lose two to three pounds when you dress them. Another reason is that if you fillet the breasts, there's no need to clean out the body cavity. How

you should handle a bird may also depend on whether you intend to preserve all or part of it for your trophy room—more on that later. For now, let's deal with the edible parts.

The wild turkey is arguably our most delicious game bird. However, meat quality

## HOW TO SCORE A TURKEY

The National Wild Turkey Federation maintains official records of wild turkeys taken by fair-chase methods anywhere in the world. Their scoring system consists of a combination of three measurements, as follows: Score = (weight) + (2 x beard length) + (10 x [right spur length + left spur length]).

Weight is measured to the nearest ounce on a certified scale. Though not required, live weight is recommended, as it yields a higher score. Measure the beard from the center point where it protrudes from the skin to the end of the longest bristle. Bristle length tends to be fairly uniform on an individual beard, but you may have one or two that are noticeably longer. Pay particular attention for these, as they will boost your score. Occasionally, a bird will have more than one beard. Such toms are categorized as nontypical. In this case the combined length of all beards is summed and multiplied by two. Spur length is measured along the outside edge, from that point where the spur protrudes from the scaled leg skin to the tip of the spur. Both of the latter two measurements are made to the nearest $1/16$ inch.

Wild Turkey Records is intended not as a ranking system but a permanent record of all birds harvested by its members; there are no minimum size qualifications for entry. Official registration forms are available from the NWTF. All entries must be signed, witnessed, and mailed to the National Wild Turkey Federation, P.O. Box 530, Edgefield, SC 29824-0530. For more information and to download record forms, visit www.nwtf.org.

will depend on several things, particularly how you care for the bird after killing it. First, cool the bird down and keep it cool, especially if you plan on weighing it round (with guts intact). The fastest and easiest way to prepare a turkey is to simply fillet the breast meat off the body and remove the legs. This eliminates the need to eviscerate, skin, or pluck the bird. Some hunters even forgo the legs, which tend to yield very little meat that is also of marginal quality.

If you choose to keep the bird whole, for roasting or deep-fat frying, you will have to gut and pluck or skin it. If you field dress it, never rinse it in a stream, pond, or lake, as this could introduce harmful bacteria. Wait until you get home, and rinse the body cavity with a hose. Plucking takes more work, but leaving the skin on helps retain what little fat there is in the skin.

How you ultimately cook your bird is limited only by your own imagination. They taste great, whether roasted, baked, smoked, deep-fat fried, chicken fried; you name it.

## The Trophy Room

Before killing your bird you should have an idea whether you intend to save some or all of the turkey for mounting purposes. You have several options. In the case of a full mount, you'll want to preserve the turkey intact and in the best condition possible. Wipe or rinse off any blood immediately, and avoid ruffling the feathers, particularly those of the fan. You should carry a few cotton balls, which you can stuff in the bird's mouth to absorb any blood. Keep the bird cool until you get home. Then wrap it carefully in newspaper. Place it in a plastic garbage bag, and put it in the freezer or bring it directly to your taxidermist. Another option is a head-and-fan mount, which is attractive and economical and takes up a bit less space in the trophy room. Treat the bird in the same manner you would for a full mount.

## Skin Mount

A much cheaper alternative is a full skin mount. If you do it yourself, begin by making an incision in the skin, from the vent up to the base of the neck, where the feathers end. Then skin around the base of the neck. Carefully skin the entire bird, without further incisions if possible. Remove the wings by cutting at the shoulder joint, then cut the skin around the base of each; sew these two incisions closed. Remove any remaining flesh or fat from the skin. Rub a mixture of salt and borax into the skin. Turn it over, spread it out, and tack it to a board to dry. When the skin has dried, trim around the edges to neaten them up. You can also sew the skin onto a piece of felt, much the same as a bearskin rug.

## Fan Mount

Fan mounts are among the most popular and inexpensive ways to display your trophy. Again, you can do it yourself or take it to a taxidermist. First, remove the beard by cutting or pulling it away from the breast. Be sure to leave enough flesh at the base to keep the bristles intact. Moisten the base, and dip it in a solution of salt and borax. Then set it in a well-ventilated area to dry.

Next, cut the tail off at its base, leaving enough flesh and bone so the fan remains intact. Turn the tail over, and on the back or bottom side, carefully begin filleting the flesh away by guiding your knife blade along the shafts of the large tail feathers. You'll soon encounter a bone at the center of the fan base. Leave this intact for now.

Turn the tail over, and do the same thing on the top. You may want to leave several layers or tracts of secondary tail coverts—the smaller tail feathers—in place. If you look carefully, you will find a small fleshy appendage with several short, waxy feathers at the end. This is the tip of the oil gland. Fillet just above this and down, removing the gland and all flesh and feathers below it, but save this for later mounting. Now, with a pair of diagonal cutters, cut away the bone in the center of the tail base. This should leave you with a full, intact fan. Carefully remove any remaining flesh and fat, then cover the base of the quills with salt and borax.

Next, spread the fan out and fasten it to a board so that it will dry in this position. You may also want to lay it flat and place something on top of it so it remains flat. Pluck some of the shorter tail feathers from the piece you cut away earlier and set them aside for later.

Once the fan is fully dried, replace some of the shorter feathers, fastening them in place with hot glue. You can purchase game-bird fan-mount plaques at most outdoor retailers that come with slots for the fan and beard, or you can make your own. Hot-glue the beard in the bottom slot and the fan in the top slot, and hang it on the wall.

## Beards and Spurs

Some hunters prefer to save only the beards and spurs. When dressing your bird, cut

off the legs and set them aside to dry. After they have dried sufficiently, remove the spur by cutting across the leg, through the bone above and below the spur, leaving a short length of leg bone with the spur still attached. With a Q-tip, clean the marrow from inside the leg bone. You can either leave the scaly skin attached or peel it off, depending on the desired look. Then you can string the spurs on a piece of rawhide, to make a necklace or hatband.

After removing the beard and drying it, as described above, you can display it in one of several ways. One way to attractively display your beard is in the brass base of a shot shell. First, remove the plastic hull of the shell and the primer from the brass. Next, hot-glue a small loop of rawhide or cord to the base of the beard. Then pull this loop through the primer hole, pulling the base of the beard up into the brass. Glue in place, and hang on the wall. You can also hang one or more beards on a separate plaque, which you can buy or make.

■ Spurs are what really boosts a turkey's score because the length of each is multiplied by 10.

# State/Provincial Wildlife Agencies

Alabama Division of Wildlife and Freshwater Fisheries, 64 North Union Street, Suite 567, Montgomery, AL 36730; (800) 848-6887; www.dcnr.state.al.us

Arizona Game and Fish Department, 2221 West Greenway Road, Phoenix, AZ 85023; (602) 942-3000; www.azgfd.gov

Arkansas Game & Fish Commission, 2 Natural Resources Drive, Little Rock, AR 72205; (501) 223-6300; www.agfc.state.ar.us

California Department of Fish and Game, 1416 9th Street, Sacramento, CA 95814; (916) 445-0411; www.dgf.ca.gov

Connecticut Department of Environmental Protection, Wildlife Division, 79 Elm Street, Hartford, CT 06106; (860) 424-3011; www.dep.state.ct.us

Delaware Division of Fish & Wildlife, 89 Kings Highway, Dover, DE 19901; (302) 739-5297; www.fw.delaware.gov

Florida Fish and Wildlife Conservation Commission, Division of Hunting & Game Management, 2574 Seagate Drive, Suite 101, Tallahassee, FL 32301; (850) 488-4676; myfwc.com/hunting

Georgia Department of Natural Resources, Wildlife Resources Division/Game Management, 2070 Highway 278 SE, Social Circle, GA 30025; (770) 918-6416; www.georgiawildlife.com

Hawaii Division of Forestry and Wildlife, 1151 Punchbowl Street, Honolulu, HI 96813; (808) 587-0166; www.dofaw.net

Idaho Fish and Game, 600 South Walnut, Box 25, Boise, ID 83707; (208) 334-3700; (800) 554-8685; fishandgame.idaho.gov

Illinois Department of Natural Resources, One Natural Resources Way, Springfield, IL 62702-1271; (217) 782-6302; www.dnr.state.il.us/index.htm

Indiana Division of Fish & Wildlife, 402 West Washington Street, Indianapolis, IN 46204; (317) 232-4080; www.in.gov/dnr

Iowa Department of Natural Resources, License Bureau, Wallace State Office Building, Des Moines, IA 52309; (515) 281-8688; www.iowadnr.com

Kansas Department of Wildlife and Parks, 512 SE 25th Avenue, Pratt, KS 67124; (620) 672-5911; www.kdwp.state.ks.us

Kentucky Department of Fish & Wildlife Resources, #1 Sportsman's Lane, Frankfort, KY 40601; Licenses by phone: (877) 598-2401; www.fw.ky.gov

Louisiana Department of Wildlife & Fisheries, Wildlife Division, P.O. Box 98000, Baton Rouge, LA 70898-9000; (225) 765-2846; www.wlf.louisiana.gov

Maine Department of Inland Fisheries and Wildlife, 41 State House Station, Augusta, ME 04333-0041; (207) 287-8000; www.maine.gov/ifw

Maryland Department of Natural Resources, Wildlife and Heritage Division, 201 Baptist Street, Salisbury, MD 21801; Southern Region (301) 743-5161; Western (301) 777-2136; Central (410) 836-4557; Eastern (410) 543-6595; www.dnr.state.md.us

Massachusetts Division of Fisheries and Wildlife; 1 Rabbit Hill Road, Westborough, MA 01581; (508) 389-6300; www.mass.gov/dfwele/dfw

Michigan Department of Natural Resources, Wildlife Division, Box 30444, Lansing, MI 48909-7944; (517) 373-1263; www.michigan.gov/dnr

Minnesota Department of Natural Resources, 500 Lafayette Road, St. Paul, MN 55155-4001; (888)-MINNDNR (888-646-6367); www.dnr.state.mn.us

Mississippi Department of Wildlife, Fisheries and Parks, 1505 Eastover Drive, Jackson, MS 39211; (601) 432-2400; www.mdwfp.com

Missouri Department of Conservation, Wildlife Division, Box 180, Jefferson City, MO 65102-0180; (573) 751-4115; mdc.mo.gov

Montana Fish, Wildlife and Parks; 1420 East Sixth Avenue, P.O. Box 200701, Helena, MT 59620-0701; (406) 444-2535; www.fwp.mt.gov

Nevada Department of Wildlife, 1100 Valley Road, Reno, NV 89512; (775) 688-1500; www.ndow.org

Nebraska Game and Parks Commission, 2200 North 33rd Street, Lincoln, NE 68503; (402) 471-0641; www.ngpc.ne.gov

New Hampshire Fish and Game Department, 11 Hazen Drive, Concord, NH 03301; (603) 271-2461; www.wildlife.state.nh.us

New Jersey Division of Fish & Wildlife, Box 400, Trenton, NJ 08625-0400; (609) 292-2965; www.njfishandwildlife.com

New Mexico Department of Game and Fish, Box 25112, Santa Fe, NM 87504; (505) 476-8000; www.wildlife.state.nm.us

New York State Department of Environmental Conservation license sales office, 625 Broadway, Albany, NY 12233-4790; www.dec.state.ny.us/website/dfwmr/ wildlife/guide

North Carolina Wildlife Resources Commission, Division of Wildlife Management, 1722 Mail Service Center, Raleigh, NC 27699-1722; (919) 707-0050; www .ncwildlife.org

North Dakota Game and Fish Department, 100 North Bismarck Expressway, Bismarck, ND 58501-5095; (701) 328-6300; www.gf.nd.gov

Ohio Division of Wildlife, 1840 Belcher Drive, Columbus, OH 43224; (614) 265-6300; www.dnr.state.oh.us

Oklahoma Department of Wildlife Conservation, P.O. Box 53465, Oklahoma City, OK 73152; (405) 590-2584; www .wildlifedepartment.com

Oregon Department of Fish and Wildlife, 3406 Cherry Avenue NE, Salem, OR 97303; (503) 947-6000; www.dfw.state .or.us

Pennsylvania Game Commission, 2001 Elmerton Avenue, Harrisburg, PA 17110-9797; (717) 787-4250; www.pgc.state .pa.us

Rhode Island Division of Fish and Wildlife, 277 Great Neck Road, West Kingston, RI 02892; License Division: (401) 222-3576; www.dem.ri.gov

South Carolina Department of Natural Resources Licensing, Box 167, Columbia, SC 29202; (803) 734-3838; www.dnr .sc.gov

Tennessee Wildlife Resources Agency, Information & Education Division, Box 40747, Nashville, TN 37204; (615) 781-6500; www.state.tn.us/twra

Texas Parks & Wildlife Department, 4200 Smith School Road, Austin, TX 78744; (512) 389-4505; www.tpwd.state.tx.us

Utah Division of Wildlife Resources, P.O. Box 146301, Salt Lake City, UT 84114-6301; (801) 538-4700; www.wildlife.utah .gov

Vermont Fish & Wildlife Department, 103 South Main Street, Waterbury, VT 05671-0501; (802) 241-3700; www.vtfis handwildlife.com

Virginia Department of Game and Inland Fisheries, Wildlife Division, 4010 West Broad Street, Box 11104, Richmond, VA 23230-1104; (804) 367-1000; (866) 721-6911; www.dgif.virginia.gov

Washington Department of Fish and Wildlife, 600 Capitol Way North, Olympia, WA 98501-1091; Licensing: (360) 902-2464; Wildlife Program: (360) 902-2515; wdfw.wa.gov

West Virginia Division of Natural Resources, Wildlife Resources Section, Capitol Complex Building 3, Charleston, WV 25305; (304) 558-2771; www.wvdnr .gov

Wisconsin Department of Natural Resources, Bureau of Customer Services and Licensing, Box 7921, Madison, WI 53707; (608) 266-2621; (800) 282-0367; www.dnr.state.wi.us

Wyoming Game and Fish Department, 5400 Bishop Boulevard, Cheyenne, WY 82006; (307) 777-4600; gf.state.wy.us

## CANADA

Alberta Environment, 9915 108 Street, Edmonton, Alberta T5K 2G6; (780) 944-0313; environment.alberta.ca

British Columbia Ministry of Environment, Fish and Wildlife Branch, P.O. Box 9374, Stn Prov Govt., Victoria, BC V8W 9M4; Canada (800) 663-7867; local (250) 387-9771; www.env.gov.bc.ca/fw/index.html

Manitoba Conservation, Wildlife Branch, Box 42, 200 Saulteaux Crescent, Winnipeg, Manitoba R3J 3W3; (800) 214-6497; (204) 945-6784; www.gov.mb.ca/conservation

Ontario Ministry of Natural Resources, 300 Water Street, Box 7000, Peterborough, ON K9J 8M5; (800) 667-1940; www.mnr .gov.on.ca

Ministère des Ressources naturelles et de la Faune du Quebec, 880, ch. Sainte-Foy, Quebec, QC G1S 4X4, (418) 627-8691, ext. 7384; www.mrnf.gouv.qc.ca/english/home.jsp

# Patterning Target

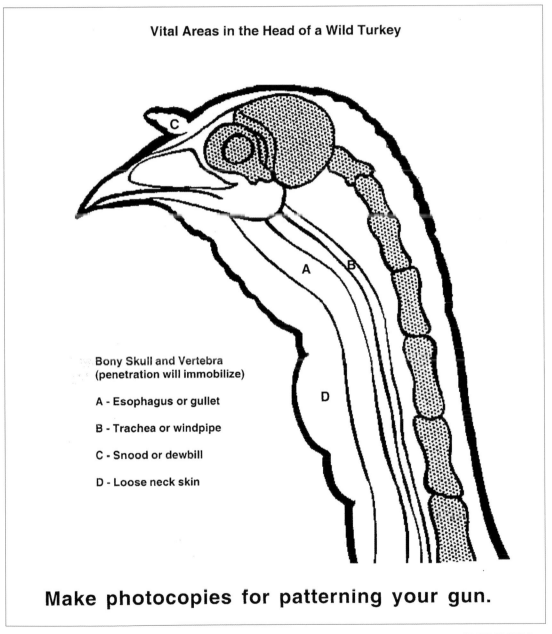

**Vital Areas in the Head of a Wild Turkey**

Bony Skull and Vertebra
(penetration will immobilize)

A - Esophagus or gullet

B - Trachea or windpipe

C - Snood or dewbill

D - Loose neck skin

## Make photocopies for patterning your gun.

# Turkey Hunter's Checklist

**Vest**
- ❏ two box calls
- ❏ two slates, synthetic material
- ❏ diaphragms
- ❏ ziplock bag
- ❏ strikers
- ❏ shock call, owl or coyote
- ❏ gobble tube
- ❏ call-care kit—chalk, sandpaper, and scrub pads
- ❏ decoys
- ❏ stakes
- ❏ turkey wing
- ❏ flashlight
- ❏ compass
- ❏ multipurpose tool
- ❏ knife
- ❏ bottle of water
- ❏ bite-size candy bars
- ❏ toilet tissue in a ziplock bag

**Clothing**
- ❏ extra face mask
- ❏ camo gloves
- ❏ boots
- ❏ hat
- ❏ pants
- ❏ shirts
- ❏ undershirts
- ❏ poly pants
- ❏ fleece sweatshirt
- ❏ jacket
- ❏ rubber boots
- ❏ turkey boots
- ❏ raincoat
- ❏ rain pants
- ❏ rain hat

**Other**
- ❏ blind
- ❏ seat/stool
- ❏ clippers/pruners
- ❏ saw
- ❏ insect repellent
- ❏ ThermaCell
- ❏ binoculars

**Weaponry**
- ❏ shotgun
- ❏ shells

**Muzzleloader**
- ❏ gun
- ❏ shot
- ❏ powder
- ❏ quickloads
- ❏ wads
- ❏ shot cups
- ❏ primers
- ❏ cleaning kit

**Bow**
- ❏ bow
- ❏ arrows
- ❏ broadheads
- ❏ stoppers
- ❏ release

Page numbers in italics refer to illustrations.

# About the Author

Bob Humphrey is a registered Maine guide and a certified wildlife biologist with more than twenty-five years of experience hunting turkeys across North America. The author of *New England Turkey Hunting—Strategies for Success*, he has also published articles in *Petersen's Hunting* and *Outdoor Life*. He lives in Pownal, Maine.

■ The author with his daughter, Helen, and son, Ben